THE SUSTAINABLE BRAIN

An Analytical Mind's Guide to Creating a Sustainable Life

AREE BLY

ISBN: 979-8-9888082-0-6

Printed in the United States of America

YOUR FREE GIFT

Get Your Free Gift Here!

As a thank you for reading my book, I'd like to gift you a downloadable PDF workbook to help you reflect on and explore the new ideas presented to you inside this book. You can get your copy here: www.areebly.com/the-sustainable-brain-book-guide

For Lars, Jim, and Gertrud. Your footsteps, encouragement, and support literally from day one gave me the tools to lead myself well no matter which corner of the earth I explore.

TABLE OF CONTENTS

FOREWORD

A book is a collection of words. As analytical people, we like to organize things into sets and study them independently. In that sense, I think you will find the set of words in this book organized in a pattern that speaks to us analytical people about careers and, more importantly, about life. I found these words refreshing and practical.

In her down-to-earth style, Aree speaks from her experience of living the corporate life and riding the ups and downs, and then the experience of counseling others, such as myself, to help us find our way.

But for me, this book is much more than a collection of words analyzed in isolation. Because I know the person behind the words, I see that, at the core, this book is about being real about being human. Aree freely opens the windows of her life to bridge us from our corporate self to our real and whole self.

As we understand our real selves better, we recognize we must do battle with drift, allowing the natural currents and patterns to take us places without asking the difficult questions. As analytical individuals, we understand drift as a parameter that we can model. Aree understands it as a human reality that must be monitored. Following drift can be an easy default path, but it likely leads to burnout, not growth. This book will give you the tools and awareness to avoid this trap.

Aree recognizes that we humans are not machines that can crank through problems without purpose or plan over the long term. She sees the big picture of our lives and is preparing us for the long-term journey, not next quarter's sprint. Like a well-planted tree, we have an opportunity to experience long-term sustainable growth that can bear much fruit.

The Sustainable Brain is the nourishment for your mind to make that growth a reality.

Dave Kester, *Founder of Coaching Actuaries*

INTRODUCTION

I have an analytical mind. It is why I went into and found success in an actuarial career. My analytical mind takes the lead in most situations. It is my go-to approach to understanding the world. I collect facts. I seek out patterns.

When it comes to finding our way in life, though, the common advice is to follow our passions or listen to our inner voice. Unfortunately, I think mine either speaks way too softly or I'm not familiar with the language it is speaking. Because I cannot make out what that voice is saying.

However, I do know how to use some of my strengths. I do know how to seek out patterns in the facts in front of me.

Growing up and in my early career, I took a few different approaches to deciding which path to take. The two approaches are what I would now call following and drifting.

I started out as a follower. I blame birth order. I was the second of two children. When I was young, our family moved often. We lived in seven homes in five different states before I graduated from high school.

The one constant as we moved around all that time was my family. And for me as an introverted little sister, the most important person in the family was my brother. He was outgoing, entertaining, and quick to make friends. I was everything opposite of that... shy, a wallflower, and more reserved. Although we were opposites, we got along very well. As I was only a year behind him in school, I effortlessly fell into the younger sister role. He lived large and I tagged along as often as he would let me. His friends became my friends. Luckily, he was generous with his time, his energy, and his attention.

Although we were different in personality, we were very similar academically. We both excelled in math. We both took our education seriously and were always near the top of the class. Perhaps those similarities were the main reason following in his footsteps was very easy for me. I let him blaze the trail. All I had to do was follow in lock step.

When he graduated high school at the top of his class, I knew it was time to start testing my own wing strength. It didn't seem too daunting, though. Even though he would be away at college the next year, I knew he would only be a phone call away if I needed anything. I could still watch and learn from a distance.

The universe, however, had other plans. Just a month after graduation, he was killed in a car accident. One day here, the next one gone. Just like that, I became a follower without a leader. The footsteps that I was carefully following abruptly stopped.

As much as I thought I was ready to spread my own wings, the force of having him ripped away upended me. In retrospect, I can see that the 16-year-old me did what I needed to at that point. I needed an easy path forward. So, I leaned hard on my skills and natural talents and let the current carry me where it would.

Unintentionally, I started using a new approach to navigating my career. Drifting on the current of my skills in math, it wasn't long before opportunities started showing themselves. I soon found myself head down in a math and accounting double major. It made sense given my skills. Coming out of graduate school, I stepped into the actuarial career - a perfect fit for my skills.

Luckily, the prevailing winds that created the current for that next decade or two were great. I meandered through a successful career at some truly fantastic companies. Through it all, I leaned on my skillset and waited for the next opportunity to present itself. I didn't have to do any navigating. Good things were coming my way. Promotions. Interesting projects.

Drifting was effortless, simple, and at least for a while, a fine option... until it wasn't.

What I hadn't realized was that I was slowly drifting off course. It took me a while to notice it because I was meeting so many external definitions of the word success. I had followed my skills but had lost track of myself somewhere along the way. I was just going through the motions. It was time to take the reins in my career and create something more sustainable.

Everywhere I look now and in so many conversations I have, I notice undeniable symptoms and signs of unsustainability in our careers and lives. Somehow, we have found ourselves in roles that continuously ask more and more of us... and we often oblige. In the process of meeting the various demands, and in our traditional success, we are falling into traps that take us further from being able to create lives that are sustainable in their own right. Lives that create enough energy to sustain in all the ways that we expend that energy. Lives in which we can thrive.

In short, we are not creating lives that we want to be living and we are losing our ability to find joy on the journey as a result.

When I step back and look at what is happening, three pieces of evidence leap out at me. These are symptoms of unsustainability. They are taking us out of the lives we long to enjoy. We are **burning out**, we are **checking out**, and we are afraid of being **found out**. We will explore these three elements first.

I am someone with an analytical mind, like many of you. It is exactly that same brain that powers so much of our success that can get us into traps.

That's right - I place some of the blame for unsustainability squarely on our brains.

As an analytical individual, I love my brain. I love how it finds patterns and is built for efficiency. However, its natural tendency for ease and short cuts along the way can be the root of much of the unsustainability. The analytical brain tends to fall for three traps... focusing too much on finding the **right answers**, getting stuck in a pattern of **success**, and viewing **identity** in the wrong light. Each of these is natural for our brains to do... and they put us smack dab into the unsustainable camp.

Sustainability requires seeing ourselves as a **whole** and recognizing how we are managing needed **resources**. It happens along the **journey** and not in the achievements we find at the end.

So how do we step out into a sustainable life and career? Sustainability is a valuable characteristic of a system. It allows the system to function in perpetuity. What is our life, if not an amazing system in which we - our bodies, minds, and hearts - are a beautiful and complex system?

The sustainability of any system starts with knowing the essence of the system and respecting those facts. For our personal system, that translates to **authenticity** - knowing who you are and being able to show up to the rest of the world as that person. And that takes art!

The art of authenticity, for me, is made up of three pillars. In order to step out as ourselves and let authenticity create the needed connections with others, we need to be **aligned** with who we are today, share that truth in a **relevant** manner, and use some **tact** in the process.

No sustainable system is static. It is constantly changing and moving. Our sustainability relies on constant motion as well... intentional motion. When we step out, we can do so intentionally. We are able to make **choices** and **experiment** deliberately to create what we want along the way while recognizing the impact of **external** situations around us.

Even though our brain has fallen into some traps that have led us into unsustainability, it also has the power to help us on the journey to sustainability. It can help us out of this mess! It is an integral piece, in fact.

We can unleash its superpower for finding **patterns** in the new information coming out of our experimentation, switch on the power of **motivation**, and **support our brain** as it overcomes some of the shortcuts it is currently taking. We are not looking to disconnect our brain from the system, but rather to turn it into a valuable part of the system as we create the sustainability we are missing.

My sincerest wish for you as a reader is that you are equipped with the tools to show up as you are today, able to ignite the analytical mind that has brought you success to this point and begin to thrive.

I hope this book offers you what you need to create a sustainable career and more importantly, the sustainable life you deserve to be living. One that engages you every day and creates joy and wonder with surprises around every corner.

For all my analytical-minded friends, this book provides the pieces to the puzzle that I move around daily to move myself closer to the sustainable life I strive to live. The pieces are not put together the same way for any two people. Nor are the pieces shaped the same. With an understanding of what the components are for creating your unique sustainable life, however, I believe you will be ready to start your own adventure.

There are many ways to get what you need from this book.

For those of you that want to use this as a self-help book, spend time on the "Analyze This..." section at the end of each chapter. The questions and actions offered are a way to get yourself started.

To exponentially increase the value within this book and bring it to life for yourself, I encourage you to purchase and use the companion workbook. It offers space to capture your insights and many additional reflection questions and exercises. Consider it a working journal to put these ideas into practice. More information can be found at the end of the book.

If you aren't into self-help and just love to read, by all means skip over those sections and just keep on reading.

And for those looking for something specific, go straight to whichever chapter is calling to you today.

However you choose to use it, may this book be one of many stepping stones you employ as you create a sustainable life and career.

PART 1:
UNSUSTAINABILITY

SECTION 1:
YOU'RE OUT

"You're out!" The umpire makes the call at the plate. As the runner, it is clear. You didn't get to the plate in time. You didn't beat the ball. Better luck next time.

I am a tennis player. And at the level I play, there are usually no official umpires. I get to make the calls for myself. I determine what is in and what is out. I have a clear measurement that I am watching - the bright white line. If the ball falls outside the line, it's out. If it doesn't, it is in.

Why is it not as easy to recognize when we are out in our day-to-day? Wouldn't it be great to have an umpire watching our every move and calling us out when we're off track so we can improve from there?

The reality is that we *can* see when we are out if we pay attention to the signs. Let's start with where many of us have found ourselves lately.

In talking with high performers and analytical individuals like me, it's clear that we all want to be in the game. We want to be performing at high levels and continuously improving. We have been successful at many things to this point. And we want to be creating a life that we can sustain and love living for the long haul.

So, it is both surprising and challenging when we find ourselves out.

How do we know when we are out? Just take a look in the mirror or at your team. The signs of feeling burned out, starting to check out, and being afraid of being found out are there.

Each of these "outs" is our life calling us out. And it's about time we started listening so we can get back into our life.

I have certainly found myself out in all of these manners at various points in my career. I have learned over the years to recognize them each for what they are… signals that I have crossed a line and need to make a change.

CHAPTER 1:
BURNED OUT

At some point in the life of a consultant, there's a shift from being an individual contributor and even leading projects to being a rainmaker. At least this was the case in each one of the consulting companies I worked at.

To be considered a senior member of the team, one of the competencies was the ability to bring in business. After all, for a consulting business, nobody's going to get paid if there are no clients to work with.

The very first time I was put in the position of becoming a rainmaker, I had been an actuary for many years and was very confident in my technical abilities. The organization I was with had some incredible rainmakers. They seemed to have no hesitation in calling a potential client out of the blue and starting a conversation around the challenges that they might be facing and how our team would be the solution they have been looking for.

Since that approach had worked so well for others at the firm, it was on page one of the playbook (and from what I could tell, there was only one page in that playbook). So, when my turn came to step up as a rainmaker, that was the direction I was given.

It started out reasonably well... Do some research to identify the company and person to reach out to. Make sure no one else is already working with them. Learn a little bit about the potential client so you can ask intelligent questions.

And then I would start to stress. I hated the next step. It took a ton of self-talk, practicing what I would say, and numerous false starts dialing the phone. I could not find a big enough treat to reward myself with if I could just complete ten of these calls this week. Why was it so hard to just pick up the dang phone and start a conversation?

Playing by this playbook was killing me!

But the most challenging part was the impact it had on the rest of my work. After expending all my mental and emotional energy on gearing up for these ultimately unsuccessful calls, I didn't have anything left of quality to give to the rest of my work.

I had unwittingly crossed the line into an early stage of burnout.

I wasn't alone then, and I still see it happening all around me now.

One of the most dynamic actuaries I have met – and for those of you that know actuaries, you might be wondering whether a dynamic actuary even exists… they do – came to me recently because they were burning out. Ryan explained that early in their career, they were the personification of the Energizer Bunny. There was no way to slow them down. Whether it was flying out weekly to spend time with clients or racing their mountain bikes in wild terrain, they were always on the go. They loved the thrill of the chase and the excitement of a deep conversation on a new finance product. They drew their energy from interactions with others and were creating an amazing consulting career for themselves.

> *We are (rightly) so connected between our occupations and our personal lives that burnout can happen in ANY area and has repercussions in EVERY area of our lives.*

And here they were, seemingly on empty. There was no excited lilt in their voice. They were sitting still as they recounted their challenges.

Facing burnout came as a surprise to them and their close friends that saw the shift. The company they had been working for had recently been acquired. An event like this is usually rife with newness and opportunity, all of which typically energize them. Yet they were unable to light the fire in this new environment.

Of course, I jumped at the chance to be their partner in dissecting their current burnout and reclaiming the energized life they used to lead. What struck me first was the fact that if they can get burned out – the Energizer Bunny themselves - there is not a person on this planet that is immune. It's no wonder that we've got an epidemic right now.

While people feel burnout differently, there are some common dimensions of burnout and reasons for them.

Dimensions of Burnout

As the name implies, burnout is very much about energy and expending our resources inefficiently. When we have burned out all of our resources, we are left with nothing but a pile of ashes. We've spent every last drop. We have come to the end of our supply.

The World Health Organization offers this burnout definition: "a syndrome conceptualized as resulting from chronic workplace stress that has not been successfully managed." It is now included in the International Classification of Diseases as an occupational phenomenon.

As I've come to learn, though, it is not isolated to our occupations. We are (rightly) so connected between our occupations and our personal lives that burnout can happen in ANY area and has repercussions in EVERY area of our lives.

According to Christina Maslach, a professor of psychology emerita at the University of California, burnout as a syndrome is characterized by three dimensions. The first dimension is what often comes to mind because it is connected with physical energy. It is the feeling of exhaustion or being completely physically depleted. We have run out of energy to do what we are trying to do.

The second dimension comes through the emotional distance from our jobs. It can be seen in the feelings of negativity or cynicism related to what we are doing. When we are experiencing burnout in this dimension, we cannot be positively emotionally connected with what we are doing. This dimension is tied to how we view the journey we are on and the values that we can live by. As I learned through conversations with Ryan, this was the primary dimension of burnout that they had been feeling.

Professional efficacy, or the inability to perform effectively, is the third dimension. For analytical individuals and those who have achieved significant success in their careers, it can be very hard not to perform at the levels that we feel we are capable of and have achieved in the past. This is what happened to me when I burned out through the ineffective rainmaking process I found myself trying to follow.

Each of these dimensions comes into play in full-blown burnout. Congratulations…when you are experiencing all three of these dimensions, you can be clinically identified as suffering from burnout. You have hit the trifecta of physical, emotional, and mental depletion. The goal is, of course, not to get to that point.

The goal is to recognize when any one of these is starting to take hold so you can take appropriate actions to move back toward an engaged and sustainable life.

The road between a fully engaged, sustainable career and life and one in which we are suffering from full-blown burnout crosses through these three dimensions. They don't show up in any order. Interestingly enough, it has been found that disengagement - i.e., cynicism - is the one that looks and feels most like full-blown burnout. Perhaps that is because it is the hardest one to walk yourself back from.

Before we learn how to come out of burnout, it helps to understand what kind of situations can put us in these various dimensions.

Mismatches in Burnout

Let's look closer at what is happening when we are experiencing each of these burnout dimensions. There are often mismatches between what our sustainable system (i.e., life) requires and what is provided by the situation in which we find ourselves.

Whether we are consciously aware of them or not, we all have aspirations and preferred ways of living our lives. These include how we want to spend our time, how we would like to be treated, and what impact we want to have in the world.

Mismatches between the reality of our situations and the aspirations we have set in each of these areas can create feelings of overwhelm, inefficacy, and cynicism that build up to burnout.

Closing these gaps will reduce the likelihood of developing burnout and move us toward sustainability.

How we want to spend our time

One of the top complaints I received from people when researching this book is that they have too many priorities. Between our work, our home, our personal goals, and even our hobbies, there are many demands on our time.

We are becoming overwhelmed by underwhelming things.

We have become one with the hustle culture. The crown of busyness is one that we wear with pride daily. It has become our go-to response in idle small talk.

How many times do you hear some version of the following interaction in the carpool line, at the grocery store, or even at your dining room table (if you have enough time to sit down for food, that is)?

"Hey! Great to see you. How are you doing?" "Ahh… so busy! Just keeping my head above water. You?"

Being busy has become an excuse for not being well.

It isn't simply the busyness that is creating the mismatch in how we want to spend our time. If you were to make a list of things that are a priority in your life, what would it include? Would it have quality time with your family? Working on impactful projects at work?

How many of these priorities are showing up on your "what I spent my time doing today" list?

We are becoming overwhelmed by underwhelming things.

We feel less in control of our time. We have said yes to too many things that we now regret. We feel obligated by the long list of "shoulds" and "justs" that have needled their way into our to-do lists.

In the end, we have a growing gap between where our true priorities lie and where our time is actually spent.

Starting out in my career, it seemed pretty simple. There was a short list of things I needed to do for work. And there was a short list of things I needed to do for my personal life. Like a good Venn diagram, there were even areas where the two overlapped. I could find simple ways that would help me move forward on both fronts.

As my career grew and my personal life became richer and fuller, I found the priorities piling up. My neat little Venn diagram was starting to look more like a spirograph. There were so many circles of things going on. It became impossible to get everything done efficiently and effectively. All of a sudden (you know, over decades), my time had stopped being my own.

How we would like to be treated

It is in our human nature to seek out challenges. We'll talk about this more when we start digging into our choices and motivations. For now, let's consider that through these challenges, we have a vision (whether conscious or not) of what we would like to see as an outcome.

Be it appreciation, money, or even the reward of simply feeling good about what we have done, there is a give-and-take expectation. It may just be Newton's third law coming into play in our actions. We put something in, something comes back toward us.

When we perceive a gap between what we have put in and what we are getting back, it can and does impact our mental focus and our emotional state. The greater the gap, the less motivated we may become to continue on the path we are on. Lower motivation to work hard then results in poorer quality of work. Welcome to the downward spiral!

We are also not looking at what we received in a vacuum. We compare our "reward" to what others receive for what we believe is similar work.

Fairness has been with us since the first Thanksgiving table. "Mom! He got a bigger piece of the pie than I did!" If there is a gap in our perception of the fairness, we will quickly become more cynical and emotionally removed from what we are doing.

The impact that we want to have in the world.

The community we operate in and our social networks are integral components of our wellness. This is true for introverts as well as extroverts. The relationship you seek with the world around you and the impact you strive to make may be big or small. It is unique to you and evolves throughout your life.

At the core of this relationship with the world are our core values. These define what is most important to us. We hope to both see them reflected in our communities and be able to influence how they show up.

Some of the deepest cutting gaps are those that happen between our core values and the values that are exhibited in certain situations. When these gaps appear, they impact our ability to show up authentically to build those strong connections.

We begin to feel emotionally distant not only from those around us but often from our own selves.

To some degree, each one of us seeks to be a part of something bigger. These relationships and connections to the bigger world are critical to our energy and our well-being.

Noticing Burnout

What's interesting about all of these gaps is that they don't show up all of a sudden. We may notice them all of a sudden, but they grow slowly.

It's kind of like walking over to the edge of a cliff. We don't think of the 100 steps that moved us from a very safe distance far away from the cliff to the edge of the cliff as dangerous. But each step was moving us closer to that precipice.

I recently saw a sign at a candy shop that said, "In case of fire, freak out and run like hell!"

That's the mentality many of us have regarding burnout. If we're not burned out, we are fine. Sure, I can see the cliff. But I haven't fallen off it yet. I'm sure it'll be fine. Right? I'll just stand here at the edge of the cliff looking over the brink.

Don't you remember the cartoons we used to watch on Saturday mornings?!? The edge of the cliff always breaks off and hurtles Wile E. Coyote into the abyss. We can never be too sure where the "safe" part of the cliff's edge is.

It's important that we address the drivers of burnout immediately as they start showing up.

What we tend to do is push ahead until we notice ourselves on the brink of full-blown burnout. At that point, if we are lucky, we let up on the throttle a little bit. Just enough that we don't go flying off the cliff. We find that gray zone where we might still feel the heat, but we feel okay about it because we are not pushing so hard that we are fully burning out.

But even a slow burn can burn you out.

We are not going to grow in the underlying feeling of "meh" in this gray zone. The best we can do is maintain.

Wobbling on the edge of the precipice does not exactly qualify as a sustainable place to exist. Let's create better for ourselves.

Burnout is a career killer. But more importantly, it is a sustainability killer. Whether it's a slow burn or a fast burn, it takes away our engagement, our effectiveness, and our energy.

We become less confident in our performance. We become more distant from those around us both at work and at home.

When I was young, I didn't think I could burn out.

I had a lot fewer demands on my time. Yes, I was in a very demanding career - one that often took well over 40 hours of my attention each week. Even layering on top of that studying for actuarial exams, I enjoyed a lifestyle that did not include caring for children or too many other responsibilities outside of work and progressing in my job.

I could easily recharge my batteries through a night out with friends or join a volleyball league to socialize and get some physical exercise. All of these tended to sufficiently recharge my batteries.

Perhaps this put the wrong idea in my head. I wasn't watching for the danger because I had the false sense that I was immune to it.

Where my burnout tended to spring from later in my career, as you may have guessed by my spirograph of a Venn diagram, was from trying to do too much and juggling too many priorities.

What drivers do you see contributing to the burnout you are feeling?

Burnout has a significant impact on our ability to create sustainability. It can also lead us to other ways of being out. The next one is checking out.

Analyze This...

1. Looking back on the past three months, which dimension of burnout – physical, mental, or emotional – has been most prominent for you?

2. What common themes do you see as drivers leading up to your most recent feeling of burnout?

3. What activities or practices have you engaged in that help you manage stress and prevent any type of burnout?

4. If you were a superhero, what superpower would help you prevent your unique burnout?

CHAPTER 2:
CHECKED OUT

I both come from and have shaped a family that loves board games. Although I have to admit that Monopoly is the one I have a love-hate relationship with.

It likely goes back to some of my earliest experiences with the game. I distinctly remember playing with my brother and my uncle multiple times. They are both very competitive and fairly cutthroat (lovingly, I am sure) by nature. I, on the other hand, tend toward collaboration. So, the whole concept of Monopoly that requires me to out-negotiate other players to get the properties I need is nowhere near my wheelhouse.

What usually happened in these games is they would land on one of my properties and not have enough money to cover the rent. To keep the game going and enjoy the time together, I would give them a pass. "No worries...here's a blanket for your little dog. Just pay a little extra next time you land here." As soon as the tables were turned, I was out of the game faster than you can say "go to jail." Eventually, that pattern took some of the fun out of the game for me.

So, when I found myself sitting around the table with my husband and daughter playing recently, I was surprised to see how this history was causing me to check out unintentionally. At some point in the game, I started shying away from the negotiation process. It wasn't that they were being excessively competitive or cutthroat. I just wasn't finding the fun in the game anymore, maybe feeling the deep-seated personal friction of the game for myself, and I started checking out.

I did not leave the game. But I did stop playing the game. I still rolled the dice. I still moved my wheelbarrow. I paid rent where needed. I collected rent when someone landed on my properties. But I stopped looking for the fun parts. I stopped wanting to win. In fact, I was just biding my time until I could slip out and read a book.

This is one version of checking out that I envisioned when I started seeing this phenomenon in the workplace. Sometimes we're doing what's necessary... without enjoyment. We're going through the motions... without being in the game.

Nobody wants to play that version of the game. Not the person checking out, nor the other players on the board.

Just look at recent headlines about "the great resignation" or "quiet quitting." Whatever name we've put to it, checking out is happening. These are two of the forms it tends to take.

Quiet Quitting

Quiet quitting is a new term for an old issue. It is typically associated with work when we are putting in minimal effort to get through the workday. It can also happen at home just as easily.

We do not qualify as committed simply because we are still in motion.

Before we make the blanket statement categorizing it as bad or good, let's take a minute to understand what may be driving it.

As in my admittedly embarrassing approach to Monopoly recently, quiet quitting can be an intentional - though potentially subconscious - stop to playing the game. It is pushing the autopilot button and disengaging from anything more. We do this to convince ourselves that we are still in the game even though our hearts may not be fully in it.

Have you heard the saying that not making a choice IS making a choice? The same goes for committing to play the game. Quietly quitting the game is choosing not to commit to the game.

Are you committed to what is in front of you or have you committed to checking out?

When quiet quitting, we may not realize that we are checked out. Some movement is still happening. We are still completing the tasks that are required of us for the job.

We do not qualify as committed simply because we are still in motion.

When we aren't regularly committing to our job, our relationship, or whatever is in front of us, we slip into autopilot mode. But we are not engaged. Autopilot is a form of checking out.

Underlying this type of quiet quitting is the disengagement that we saw in burnout. Even at a slow burn, this disengagement is not sustainable. We cannot maintain quiet quitting for long without repercussions.

Quiet quitting can also reflect the boundaries we set around a situation. We identify what we are willing to do and what we will not do, defined in terms of activities, time, or energy. By defining and sticking to these boundaries without clearly articulating them for ourselves and others, we are quietly framing where we will be active and where we "quit" working.

These can be healthy boundaries, in which we are still engaged within the boundaries we have set.

In this situation, we may very well be fully engaged in the work we are doing when we are doing it. This can be a healthy setting of boundaries. We are at lower risk of burning out because we are engaged within the boundaries we have set.

While it does have a concerning potential impact on others, it has a lower chance of negatively impacting sustainability. The only thing making it a detrimental form of quiet quitting may be the fact that we have not made others aware of our boundaries.

Setting a healthy boundary is very different from disengaging. One will lead you toward sustainability, the other away from it.

The underlying disengagement is the aspect that creates unsustainability.

The impact of quiet quitting on those around us can range from not enjoying the game as much because of the energy that the checked-out individual is (or is not) bringing to having to shoulder the burden of someone else's checking out.

Sometimes the kindest action we can take is to be clear. Once we know what is causing us to check out, we can have the difficult conversations (with yourself and those around you) to make the changes necessary.

As we recognize that we are quiet quitting, especially with underlying disengagement, we can see it as a sign or a message to ourselves that we need a change. There is something unsustainable in the current situation that needs to be addressed.

If your situation is not engaging you, simply making it a smaller part of your day or reducing the energy you are putting toward it will not create engagement. It is time to step back and reassess.

When quiet quitting is a sign of disengagement or impending burnout, whether physical, mental, or emotional, it is worth diving in a little deeper.

If you notice quiet quitting happening, the question you should be asking yourself is why. What am I looking for?

Is your quiet quitting a reflection of disengagement or is it a reflection of boundaries that you have set?

Quiet quitting can be the precursor to a louder form of checking out.

Job Hopping

At some point, we end up beyond quiet quitting and in the very out loud and very deliberate quitting.

This is the traditional definition of quitting. Whether it's the gracefully worded resignation letter, the slamming door while we yell "I quit!", or something in between, there is nothing ambiguous about checking out of the current situation. We are walking away now. Moving on to new pastures.

> *We drift along hoping that a better situation will present itself.*

We have realized that something does not fit. We recognize that we're no longer enjoying the game. We believe that our pot of gold lies somewhere else.

And so, we quit. We check out.

The grass is greener in the next company. Or working for a different manager. Or in a different industry.

Just look at the number of people that are changing jobs every year. Especially in the latest years as we have been dealing with a pandemic. More and more people are recognizing that something needs to change and are taking action. That action is often resigning.

Sometimes all you know is where you are not a good fit and that there has to be something better out there.

But what happens when we check out and jump to a new situation without taking the time to understand what we want? We run away from the situation that we were in, and we are not concerned about where we might land.

We may end up in a serial checking-out phase.

I know many people that seem to be changing roles and companies every few years. It makes me wonder whether they are clear on what they want and whether it is something they will ever find. Will they ever land in the pasture that has just the right shade of green? It might be a wild goose chase.

We may only know that what we have is not what we want. So, we are checking out of the current situation. We drift along hoping that a better situation will present itself.

Now would be a great time to introduce one of my heroes… Hermey the Elf. Yes, the little guy who wants to be a dentist and becomes best friends with Rudolph the Red-Nosed Reindeer. He knew in his heart of hearts that he wanted to be a dentist and not one of Santa's toy-making elves. He loved everything he knew about being a dentist. He read about molars and incisors every chance he got.

He was the first example in my young life of someone checking out. Couldn't he be a dentist where he was at? Was he being pushed to fit the mold of being a toy-making elf?

What did he do? He quit. He and his best buddy Rudolph walked away from all of the naysayers. He knew all along where he was heading to, even if he didn't know how to get there.

Wouldn't it be great if we all knew where we were headed? The first step in checking back in is knowing what we want to check in to. We'll talk more about the idea of stepping into what you want shortly.

For those of us without such a clearcut view as Hermey, checking out through job hopping is our best hope. We hope that the next opportunity will be the right one. If we are lucky, we will stumble on the right fit role.

But if we don't change what we are looking for, and we don't ask ourselves questions to understand why we are checking out in the first place, we are likely doomed to repeat ourselves.

Remember that sign hanging in the candy shop? In case of fire… freak out and run like hell! The worst time to seek out a greener pasture is when the wildfire is speeding across your current pasture. At that point, you are just looking to save your life.

The best time is when you can do it deliberately and intentionally, thoughtfully aligning it with what you want (or want to experiment with) in your next situation.

Think about it. Of all the times you jumped to a new situation just to escape your current bad fit, how many times did you find that the grass was greener?

You are playing roulette with your future. When quitting because you're feeling the heat of the fire, you don't always make the best decisions about what you choose next.

The crux of this is that when we check out, we've either given up on finding (in the case of quiet quitting) or we are hoping to find (when job hopping) what we're looking for. The key in both of these situations is finding. Not creating.

Checking out is a way of giving up. It is a way of throwing up our hands and giving up control of the situation. We are choosing the easy way out.

We will have much more luck when we decide to create rather than simply find the unicorn of sustainability.

There is one more form of being out that is worth noting. And again, this one often follows burning out and checking out. It is also one that is based on fear. And that is being found out.

Analyze This...

1. If you notice yourself quiet quitting, would you categorize it more as a reflection of feelings of disengagement or of setting boundaries?

2. What impact do you see quiet quitting – either yourself or others – having on your current situation?

3. Reflect on your most recent change in role at work. Were you creating your next challenge or searching for a change?

4. If you could swap jobs with anyone in the world for a week, who would it be and why?

CHAPTER 3:
FOUND OUT

I was discovered at work. And not in the sense that I was an aspiring actress whose talent was finally noticed. Oh no, it was quite the opposite.

It was a normal Monday morning. Everybody that worked in the small office was seated around the large conference room table. I had my Starbucks chai tea in front of me. Everyone was chatting about the recent weekend with a sprinkling of work topics mixed in before the meeting started.

There was nothing special about the meeting. A standing weekly meeting to review projects, priorities, and staffing. And it was a time for office updates and highlights of what is going on in our small but close-knit office.

At this point in my career, I enjoyed leadership positions at every company where I worked. And this was no exception, as I had been hired as a director the year before.

When the whole office can fit around one table, albeit slightly snugly and elbow to elbow, there are few hard and fast rules. We didn't have an official Human Resources person setting company-wide standards. The various offices had, to date, run independently of each other.

One of the principals stood up to make an announcement. We would be shifting to formal job titles and descriptions to create consistency across offices due to continued rapid company-wide growth.

The big announcement came. "We're excited to formally recognize and extend hearty congratulations to our directors…" Three names were read off. All three of the other directors in the office. My name was left off the list. I scanned the new org chart to find my name. My title read senior actuary.

I could feel my chest tightening. I'm not used to not succeeding. I'm not used to stagnation, or worse yet slipping backward in my career. Within an hour of getting to work that day, I had been demoted.

My brain jumped into overdrive trying to make sense of this new information. Was it all a lucky run up to this point? What was this telling me about my actuarial career?

My heart silently agreed with the decision. It had been sitting on the sidelines for a while.

From the outside, there was no change other than the title. My salary stayed the same. The work I was doing stayed the same.

What changed was the fact that I had been found out. The principals of the company had noticed and called out the fact that my energy and engagement were not at the level they expected in a director.

And they were right. I wasn't fully engaged in everything they needed in a director.

What we are hiding

We might be quietly quitting as we switch to autopilot to get through the days. The mental, emotional, or physical, slow burn may be just starting or doesn't seem to be much of a problem yet.

When the truth is in the spotlight, it cannot easily be ignored.

We often go through these times not letting others know what is happening. Sometimes it is because we, ourselves, have not paid attention enough to see it. Other times, we are focusing on curating the public view without letting on what is happening backstage.

The fear of being found out is built brick by brick. Those bricks are our worries about letting others down. Fears of what will change. Uncertainty about what the future might hold.

There is something unique about being found out, which is probably at the root of why we fear it. When the truth is in the spotlight, it cannot easily be ignored. Once we face the reality of our situation, the next logical step is to deal with it.

So, what is it we're hiding? What do we hope to keep out of the spotlight?

In short, it is the truth. We are afraid of someone seeing our truth.

That truth may be our desire to do something different. Perhaps we have gotten tired of the path we're on. We're ready to try something new. Or we have reached the next season of our careers and lives.

The truth may be that we are facing challenges. We may not want to admit our struggles because it looks like everyone around us is effortlessly achieving similar things. The challenges we are facing could be leading us toward burnout or causing us to be checked out.

The truth could be that we are not committed to the path we are on. Or that we are afraid of failing.

This list could go on and on. It is different for each person.

If someone were to ask you what you are hiding, you may have the answer right away. Or maybe you can't even see the truth because you have hidden it so well from others that you are unable to see it now as well.

I, like any good analytical individual, believe that facts and data give us power. Operating with less information leads to poor results. It is a perfect example of the "garbage in… garbage out" concept. When we use information that is incomplete, inaccurate, or out of date, the outcomes of any process will be poor.

Okay, so maybe a blind squirrel does find a nut occasionally. There are times when we stumble into a good place. But that is not a solid strategy for creating sustainability.

We are leaving our happiness to a shot in the dark, at best.

The truth that we are looking for is what's happening to us right now. And being found out is one way to bring that truth to the forefront.

Who is finding out?

There are a few people that may find out your truth.

As it happened with me that Monday morning, someone else could be finding out and calling out your truth. Whether they do it publicly or while sitting down for a coffee with you, once the dust settles, you will realize it can surprisingly be a very kind act.

But before we get to that, who are these other people that might find out our truth? It could be anyone.

We want our boss to believe we are fully committed to the job and deserving of the top merit raise in the upcoming review cycle.

Our team is counting on us to be contributing members. We know that any changes we might make could have repercussions for those around us. We have a sense of responsibility to them that can be overriding the sense of responsibility and truth for ourselves.

Sometimes we are hiding from our family or those that care about us. Many well-meaning individuals have supported us in our paths. They have encouraged us emotionally and financially through the ups and downs. They are so proud of what we have achieved to date. Why would we want to let them down?

Even that Facebook non-friend who always seems to want to see you fail. Wouldn't they love it if they found out that you were struggling?

When you think of somebody finding out your secret, you may overlook yourself. You are the person who KNOWS the truth. You are not the one in the dark, right?

Well, we as humans are incredibly adept at lying to ourselves. Our brain loves to look for any evidence to support beliefs we hold tight, even if those beliefs are wrong. We tend to justify or twist the truth, and sometimes outrightly ignore it, hoping that it will go away.

The truth that I am talking about, of course, is the truth about our happiness and the sustainability of the situation we are in.

The last person we say we want to let down is ourselves, yet that's the first person many of us do let down.

We say…

This is only temporary. I will be in a better spot next year so it's OK that it's not perfect right now.

What if it doesn't work out? I couldn't handle the risk.

It's not that important. I don't want that anyway.

We can convince ourselves of pretty much anything or redirect our attention somewhere else so we don't have to see the truth sitting right in front of us.

Finding the Fears

Below the surface of the fear of being found out are many other fears. I have felt many of these pass through at various times, while some like to set up shop in my head.

The Type A and people pleasers among us may relate to the fear of not living up to expectations. Whether we have put them on ourselves, such as setting a goal to become CEO, or expectations from someone else, sometimes our personalities make us more prone to holding on to these expectations well beyond their usefulness as motivators.

We fear asking for what we want – because we don't want to appear ungrateful, are afraid of being told no, or not wanting to be different.

We fear that if we need to make a change, it is an admission that we have made a mistake along the way.

The fear of commitment might be playing a part. No, I'm not talking about the fear of committing to your significant other or making a big decision to have children. It is the commitment required to make a change once the truth is known. It's much easier to sit back and pretend that we don't have a new dream than to commit to making it a reality.

And it is the fear of leaving our comfort zone, even when it is anything but comfortable. Maybe a better term for this is fear of leaving our familiarity zone.

A final fear that is unique but can also play a part in the fear of being found out is imposter syndrome. With imposter syndrome, even when all the evidence would say otherwise, we hold on to the fear that someone will discover we are not competent or intelligent or successful.

The outcome

For those of you that have been found out, whether by coming to and owning your truth internally, or by having someone call you out, what was the result?

It can be a new doorway to authenticity, and an opportunity to start down a new path.

My guess is you were rewarded with a mix of emotional benefits once the heart palpitations subsided.

When we are found out, we can finally see the underlying fears and facts more clearly. Through that clearer lens, we can find a sense of relief.

"Whew! I said it. I can't believe it took me that long to say what I was thinking."

Or "thank goodness that is out in the open now. I didn't realize I have been holding my breath for so long."

It offers the freedom to look at the situation with a new set of eyes. Only when we can see the situation for what it truly is can we also start to see the possibilities on the horizon. We can start to see options for living in that new truth.

What I was most surprised by after being demoted was that my energy was at an all-time high. I was relieved that we could have an open conversation about what I wanted in my career. And then I was energized by being able to focus my time on the things that were most engaging for me.

All of this adds up to an ability to not only address the situation and move through it but an ability to grow from it. It can be a new doorway to authenticity, and an opportunity to start down a new path.

And those fears of not meeting expectations, letting down the team, or facing our impostor syndrome, all look a little smaller through the new lens.

When it comes to not succumbing to the fear of being found out, Hermey the elf, whom we briefly visited in the prior chapter, is the king. He hardly hesitated. He threw up his little middle finger at being found out and boldly stomped out of the room. (Okay, this didn't happen in the movie, but I think he wanted to.)

Like some of us who have the fear of being found out, Hermey had been toying with the idea of doing something different. He had even been taking the initiative to follow his curiosity and learn more about his true love, dentistry.

When his boss finally confronted him about his apparent lack of skills and lack of interest in all things toy-making, he embraced being found out. And this led him on an incredible journey as he went in search of his dream.

He wasn't worried about what the other elves would say. He wasn't worried about whether he'd be a successful dentist or not. He felt the need to at least try to chase his dream.

Even though it was a long and winding journey, ultimately, Hermey was able to capture his dream. In the end, he was the first practicing dentist in the elf community. Talk about showing up in a new way to support your old team!

Being found out may not be the worst thing after all.

We have spent the last few chapters understanding a variety of ways that we can find ourselves "out" of our careers and lives. Finding ourselves out does not mean that we're doing something wrong. It means that we need to make a change.

Feeling burned out, finding ourselves checking out, or being afraid of being found out are just symptoms of unsustainability in our careers in our lives. They are not judgments on who we are or what decisions we've made in the past.

We didn't intentionally put ourselves out. But we can intentionally move in the other direction.

Analyze This...

1. What types of situations do you feel vulnerable in? What common themes do you see in those situations?

2. Consider something that you are hoping will not be found out. What might the worst outcome be as a result of that coming to light? What might the best outcome be?

3. How do you typically react when someone else admits to struggling with a similar challenge to yours?

4. What is the most embarrassing thing that you have ever been "caught" doing at work? How did you handle that situation?

SECTION 2:
BRAIN IS NOT HELPING

In her recent book The Long Game, Dorie Clark shares the story of a self-employed consultant in Canada, Ali Davies. Although she had enjoyed a successful corporate career for 14 years, she confessed that "at about the 10-year mark, I was feeling unsettled and unhappy. I knew I wanted out but kept convincing myself to stay. I was 'successful' and [there was] fear of what that would mean for my identity if I turned my back on the conventional definition of success, and fear of it being the wrong decision."

In one short sentence, Ali summed up three traps that we, as analytical and successful individuals, easily fall into.

The right answer trap, or the belief that there is one right decision, so we take no action for fear of being wrong.

The success trap, which is our brain getting stuck on the things that have worked for us in the past. We find ourselves seeking out more of the same success hoping for the same feeling of success, or we stay put, afraid to lose what past success has brought us.

And the third trap of identity. We become very tied to who we are in our careers and what others see us doing. As a result, we become unwilling to shift to other parts of our identity.

We don't have to be at the point of wanting to get out of our careers. It can happen anytime that the current path feels unsustainable.

Luckily, Ali eventually started asking herself the questions that needed to be asked to move forward. She realized that "sometimes the stories we tell ourselves about our professional lives hold us back if we don't dissect what's going on."

What better way for an analytical person to approach this! Let's turn on our left brain and look for information, data, and evidence that tell us what's going on.

We analytical people love our brains. I know I do! Our brain is a trusted friend. It is here to help us find the right answers, keep us safe, and be the voice of reason.

Because of this relationship, we don't realize (or maybe we willfully overlook) that our brain is also lazy and wants to take as many shortcuts as possible. In the process, it can put us in danger of going down the wrong path. These traps are evidence of those dangers.

CHAPTER 4:
RIGHT ANSWER TRAP

"The need for certainty is the greatest disease the mind faces." -Robert Greene, Mastery

Anyone who has read Douglas Adams' The Hitchhiker's Guide to the Galaxy knows that the right answer is 42. End of story. Seven and a half million years of deep thought, and the answer is clear. 42. Is Adams mocking the lengths that we will go to to find THE right answer?

As someone who has followed an educational and career path focused on mathematics, actuarial science, statistics, and other analytical areas, I find a lot of comfort and joy in finding the right answer.

Through my actuarial exams, the right answers meant the difference between passing the certification exam and failing it.

The goal was to take in the information and spit out the correct answer. There was always a right and a wrong. There was not much in between.

So, it is not a surprise that in my actuarial career, I continued to look for the right answer.

Creating sustainability in a career, however, requires a very different process. Heading for the right answer implies that you have enough information to do the calculation. It implies that you are not interested in how you get there, as long as the result is the right answer. And it can trap you in the wrong mindset.

The Trap

Looking for the right answer is a hard habit to break.

Many of my coaching clients are analytically minded individuals just like myself. We are actuaries and engineers, physicians and accountants. We are people who lead with our brains before our hearts. As a result, we are some of the first to fall into the right answer trap.

One of my clients had never been in a coaching partnership before. Coaching is not therapy or counseling, nor is it mentoring. Coaching is an alliance in which the coach is there to walk alongside the client, draw out insights, and ask questions to encourage the client to think and discover answers within themselves as they choose the direction for their future.

No one coaching relationship or session is the same as another. There is no report card or grade assigned at the end of a coaching session.

During the first coaching session with this client, we had a deep discussion about what he was doing in his current role and some of the challenges he was facing. We dug into some of his current beliefs, where some of the gaps between his prior expectations for this role and his experienced reality are. We even uncovered some insights into his core values and what he required in his career to feel at ease. We had some tangible takeaways for him to start working on.

Searching for one right answer creates limitations that restrict our ability to see options and take action.

It was a winding conversation where we followed themes, got curious, and explored his situation. We did not have any agenda or goal.

Yet given his analytical mind and the deep-seated belief that there is a right answer, his final question to me in that first session was "Did I do it right?"

The goal when navigating your career and your life is not defined by right and wrong. There is no explicit algorithm that will produce the right answer. There is no one at the end holding a clipboard. No one comparing your achievements and your path to an answer key. You are fully free to create and follow whatever path you are drawn to.

Yet because of our comfort with and focus on algorithmic approaches in our day-to-day work, this is the approach we often default to.

An algorithm is a procedure for solving a specific problem by following defined steps. The result is reproducible and predictable. There is a right answer. Even with the complexity of our careers and all the potential inputs, we are prone to believing that there is a right answer – albeit a challenging one to find.

There are many risks to searching for one right answer, especially one in which the problem itself is very complex. And what is the challenge of creating a sustainable life, if not complex? There are many moving parts both in our careers and our personal lives. And there are many forces acting outside of our control. We, ourselves, are changing throughout all our experiences.

Searching for one right answer creates limitations that restrict our ability to see options and take action.

Escaping the trap

When we are looking for a single solution, or even trying to define an algorithm that will provide the right answer for any given input, we draw boundaries around where we believe the solution may reside. We restrict possibilities so we can get to the answer more efficiently.

As a result, we have limited our own creativity. We have reduced our ability to see alternative and unexpected solutions. Ironically, this limits what we can accomplish. And it has a name.

It is known as the Einstellung effect. In German, "einstellung" means "set" and in this context, it refers to a mental set. When we are even peripherally familiar with a problem and have an initial idea of where to find the right answer, we stop seeing alternatives. The blinders go on. Our brains begin to latch on to the "right" direction that we have identified and begin to discount other possibilities.

The Einstellung effect can be especially strong when we encounter a challenge similar to one we have faced in the past. We start seeking variations on solutions that worked historically.

We have been trained to seek out the right answer quickly and to move on to the next challenge. We don't notice that we might be overlooking alternatives or even failing to recognize that alternatives might exist.

So how can we combat this? Shift the focus from problem-solving to problem-finding.

Ask questions such as the following. Am I asking the right question? Is there another way to frame the problem? How might a different perspective change the problem?

Chasing the right answer can also cause us to fall into analysis paralysis. This is a situation where we continue to gather data, make calculations, and compare results because we believe there is one right answer to be found. We enter a cycle of constant searching, researching, and analyzing. We hesitate to put any final answer on paper because there is always one more thing that we need to take into account.

Because of this analysis paralysis, we fail to take any action. But hey, at least we didn't do the wrong thing… right? After all, if there is a right answer, there also has to be a wrong answer. When we choose no answer, by staying in analysis mode, we are playing it safe.

As someone who put a lot of value on getting good grades, passing exams, and finding the right answer, being wrong can be scary.

So many questions run through my head when I think I might be wrong. Who else is seeing this? What do they think? Does this mean I am a failure? Why did I not see this coming? What IS the right answer?

This might be why analysis paralysis is such a challenge for us. It is a sneaky way of bypassing the fear of failure and replacing it with the much more noble pursuit of the right answer.

In reality, I am not getting any closer to the right answer because I have made the analytical space so comfortable.

The best advice I found to battle analysis paralysis comes from the chalkboard of a journalism classroom in the mid-1980s.

GOOD ENUF!

It was written in large letters in the top corner of the chalkboard in my dad's journalism room where the college newspaper took shape every Thursday night. Yes, I said journalism… writing… English.

I was too young to get the full nuance at the time. Today, he would be happy to know that I appreciate the sentiment and humor much more. Maybe it is because I am doing more writing myself. Or maybe it is just the wisdom that comes with age.

My dad was an English and journalism professor for much of his life. One of his responsibilities as the sole journalism professor at the small college in Wyoming was guiding the students as they published the weekly newspaper for the campus.

Every Thursday night, the rest of the family knew we would not see him home for dinner and could expect to hear the front door close behind him sometime well after midnight. He and the students poured their hearts and souls into those papers. They worked late into the night to make sure it was their best product. They wanted it to be right!

Yet there always came a time when they would have to make the call. There is no such thing as perfect. It was a creative endeavor, with no right answer.

They would eventually get to the point where the paper – the content of each column, the layout of the pictures and the ads, the opinions on the editorial page – was ready to go to print. Sometimes that decision was based on their comfort with the content, most of the time it was driven by the clock on the wall.

There were errors in some issues, and other issues could have been more artfully laid out. Yet they stuck with their "Good Enuf" rule and focused on getting a good enough paper out each week. The result was an award-winning paper.

Getting in motion and staying in motion until the job was "good enuf" was a winning strategy each week. While they sought a product they could be proud of, there was no right answer at the finish line.

In my own career, I use "good enuf" as a powerful motto.

It allowed me to avoid analysis paralysis when my best move was to put a good enough solution out and move on.

For the college newspaper, "good enuf" meant good enough for that week. They could always correct any errors in the next paper.

For you, good enough can also have a time constraint. Ask yourself whether what you are working on is good enough for the next three months. In our fast-paced careers, we are constantly iterating and improving, growing and learning. If we don't take the step of putting something out there, we will never have something to iterate on and improve.

Whether that product is a report to a client, an email, or even an algorithm-based tool that we've developed, there comes a point where "good enuf" really is good enough. We get to let go of the search for the perfect or the right answer.

When we free ourselves from focusing on the endpoint, we open up the possibility of what we may find on the path.

Good enough is not about letting ourselves off the hook. It is about breaking out of the right answer trap. And it is a surprising tool for releasing the fear of failure.

No One Path

Besides limiting ourselves through our search for a right answer and putting ourselves into analysis paralysis, the final challenge of the right answer trap is that it keeps our focus on the endpoint.

Everything that we do when we start trying to solve the problem is geared towards finding that right answer. We are paying less attention to how we are getting to the right answer and can become blind to what we learn along the way.

When we free ourselves from focusing on the endpoint, we open up the possibility of what we may find on the path.

What would have happened if I had responded to my client from the beginning of this chapter with either "yes, you did this perfectly," or "no, a coaching call should look like x"?

I can guarantee that future sessions would be tainted by the desire to follow the algorithm that was indicated as "correct" during the first session, or there would be constant attempts to tweak his approach in each session until he was rewarded with the right answer.

No actual growth would happen.

We are free to define both the direction that we are headed at any point in our career and the path that we choose to take in order to move in that direction. Neither of these elements of our navigation process are fixed. Nor can they be compared to a right or wrong answer key.

By shifting the focus off of finding a right answer, we free ourselves.

Analyze This...

1. What past opportunities have you missed because you might have been too focused on finding the "perfect" solution?

2. How might your life and career be different today if you had made decisions or acted more quickly?

3. What is a phrase (like "good enuf") that may work as a reminder for you to check whether you are in a right answer trap?

4. What might happen if you replace the words "right answer" with "most interesting answer" in a current challenge?

CHAPTER 5:
SUCCESS TRAP

I know there's no award for this - and if I am wrong, please do not tell me. I once had a 643-day streak of completing lessons on the language app Duolingo.

At the beginning of the pandemic with the kids home working on their Spanish homework, it was a great way for me to brush up on my own Spanish skills. So, I set the goal of doing 15 minutes a day. And I did. I religiously turned on the application and completed the lessons every day. I looked forward to these little breaks in my day when I could immerse myself in the Spanish language.

At first, it seemed like the little owl in the app was my friend. His little celebrations of "You've just completed your first week!" and "30 days! Keep it up!" helped to keep me on track.

What I hadn't realized was that I had just been handed my first "free" sample on the road to addiction. By the time that perky little owl was congratulating me on my streak of 200 days, I was feeling the shift from looking forward to the lesson for the sake of my own enjoyment of the Spanish language to feeling like I needed to do it to keep the streak going.

I wasn't paying as much attention to what I was learning each day. Instead, I was making sure that I got the checkmark for completing that day. By the time I was a year in, I was helplessly stuck in a success trap.

Whether it becomes a compulsive addiction or it is a cycle that we don't want to break because it feels good, the success trap can impede our ability to create sustainability. It can lead us astray from our true goals for our lives.

I have noticed different ways in which the success trap can hold us in its grip. The first is similar to what I fell into with Duolingo.

Success Addiction

While it is not necessarily a destructive addiction, it is created by some of the same processes and brain functions that we see in other addictions. We create a cycle of chemical releases in our bodies. Our bodies recognize what feels like a good thing, and then seeks out more of the same.

Our bodies have been busy releasing dopamine and serotonin. Dopamine is a motivation chemical. When it is released into the bloodstream, it increases our ability to focus and can motivate us to take action. Our dopamine levels rise as we get closer to a goal and anticipate the results.

Once we achieve our goal, whether it is winning a competition, getting public recognition, or even feeling like we are part of a crowd, serotonin is released. This creates the good feeling we associate with the success.

As we stack even small success upon small success where there is an effort put in and reward received, our bodies respond and create the good feelings. Once it is over, we want to feel that again. We begin to seek out those opportunities to repeat the cycle. What worked in the past is where our brain will naturally go. Welcome to a success trap.

Heroic Individualism

Not every success trap is rooted in addiction.

Brad Stulberg, author, researcher, and coach on human performance and sustainable success, defines heroic individualism as an ongoing game of one-upmanship against yourself and others. It includes the limiting belief that measurable achievement is the only determiner of success.

It is getting caught in the trap of always focusing on the next success. As soon as we finish notching our belt with the latest win, we look up to spot the next goal on the horizon. We are buffeted by the accumulating pile of successes behind us. Obviously, we are doing something right, right? I mean, look at all that we have accomplished.

We never really stop to enjoy what those successes have brought us, nor do we pause to understand how we might have changed through our pursuit of that last success. Instead, we look for the next, slightly higher goal.

The desire for more and the need to keep up our pace can be detrimental to our well-being and our sustainability. We may not notice potential forks in the road that could lead to more aligned pursuits for who we are today.

Even if we notice the fork in the road, we may opt to ignore it. What will others think if we veer off our path of apparent success? What if they found out that we were even thinking about shifting? As we discussed earlier, these feelings can very easily keep us from making any change. We are too busy proving to ourselves and others that we can keep this success train running.

Although we are successful ... we still feel unsatisfied.

Falling prey to heroic individualism may be due to what researchers call the hedonic treadmill. The hedonic treadmill is the tendency to remain at a stable level of happiness despite achieving our goals. We desire to be happier, and we see a path to that happiness. It is tied to our next success. Yet our happiness never remains elevated for the long term.

How many times have you heard someone say or even said something yourself along the following lines?

When I get my promotion, I will have made it!

As soon as I have my college debt paid off, I will be comfortable with my financial situation.

I will be so happy once I finally have a published article.

And what happens when that milestone is met? The happiness, the relief, or the comfort is short-lived. Within days, we find ourselves reverting to our original level of happiness.

Our minds are very good at adapting to new circumstances. Once we get that promotion, it doesn't take long before we stop feeling the pleasure that came with that achievement, and we start feeling unsettled or looking ahead to the next thing.

Although we are successful - we have gotten that promotion, paid off our college, and we have published the article - we still feel unsatisfied.

We feel trapped on the treadmill in our pursuit of the next success. Success is somewhere in the future. And because we have tied our happiness to that success, our happiness is also always in the future.

Performance Punishment

What happens to the best performers in your organization? What I often observe is that they are given more to do. They are given more responsibility. They are given new challenges to work their magic on. In short, they are given a chance to show that they can do even more!

There's a term for this when it gets out of hand. It is performance punishment. And it is yet another type of success trap.

Our natural drive for status is fueled by the accomplishments that we are able to create in our careers. Our bodies deliver feel-good chemicals when we receive accolades from those around us, even when it is in the form of offering more work to do.

Our past performance is a signal that we are capable. The tendency of those around us, especially our managers or colleagues, to come to us because they know we can produce positive results combined with the inner cycle of our reward system puts us at the risk of getting trapped in performance punishment.

We want to say yes to the new work because it will feed our desire for those feel-good chemicals. Once we say yes, we push hard and enjoy the rewards at the end. This cycle can continue until we realize that we are at risk of burnout or that we have strayed far from the path that we would actually like to be on - a sustainable and fulfilling career.

Meanwhile, as performance punishment is happening for the best performers, the rest of the team may be hoping for opportunities to test their mettle. With more of the growth opportunities going to a smaller number of individuals, we are limiting the rest of the team's and organization's potential for growth.

Now this does not mean that leaders should not reward those who are doing great things. We should, however, remain cognizant of the potential for creating a success trap. When we're asking top performers to keep pushing harder, and not checking in to make sure that is what they want, we are setting everyone up for failure.

Heroic individualism can be our own self-imposed performance punishment. We are constantly demanding more of ourselves than what it took for the prior success. We don't stop to ask whether there is another way to approach the challenge, or if this is still the right direction to be heading in. We take the continued success as a sign that we are on the right track.

The speed at which we create our own trap increases when we also have a self-sufficiency bias. This is the bias that has us saying "I created the prior success, so I am capable of doing it again." We hesitate to bring others in, whether we don't want to share the limelight, are unsure whether they will be capable, or don't want to invest time in bringing them up to speed.

Breaking out of a success trap is a challenge no matter which type of trap you are caught in - success addiction, heroic individualism, performance punishment, or any other variety. The common themes in success traps are that we tie ourselves to accomplishment-focused successes, allow our hard-wired feel-good system to drive our decisions, and fail to step back enough to gain the perspective needed to see the traps.

Not everyone falls into a success trap.

I recently had the honor of sharing some ideas on creating a sustainable career with a classroom full of actuarial students and members of a business fraternity at Drake University.

During our conversations, I asked how they define success. The first responses fell in line with what I was expecting. For actuaries, success defined by passing the next exam is front and center. And for college students in general, success can mean landing a prime summer internship. Or graduating with high honors.

And then came the surprise. A student in the middle of the room raised his hand. He said "When I feel like I'm successful at something, it's because I can look at it with a feeling of joy. If I got there on a path that makes me happy, I call that a success."

For him, the success was not driven by the achievement at the end of the path. It was defined by the feelings he created along the way.

By keeping that definition of success, he has already discovered one of the keys to releasing the hold of the success traps.

Analyze This...

1. When was the last time that you celebrated a win that no one else was aware of?

2. What challenge are you avoiding because you may be uncertain whether you can achieve it?

3. Looking at the success that you have achieved to date, who do you think you would be if no one knew about that success?

4. If you had to choose between being the world's most successful person or the world's happiest person, which would you choose? What definition of success are you using in that comparison?

CHAPTER 6:
IDENTITY TRAP

Our culture might be partly to blame for this trap. The first question we ask when we meet someone is often "What do you do?" And the answer usually is a recitation of our job title or our profession.

I am the chief this or that. I am a firefighter. I am an engineer. Or even, when being open and vulnerable, I am unemployed.

When someone asks what we do, we answer with who we are. The sentence starts with "I am..."

For decades, I answered that question with "I am an actuary" with no hesitation.

If you had told me at the beginning of my career as an actuary that I would one day voluntarily give up the letters after my name, I would have thought you were insane. And then I would try to envision what type of insanity would have had to have taken over my being for that to be true.

Yet here we are... a few decades after I went through countless hours of studying, reading, practicing, reciting, and banging my head against a wall, through which I earned that coveted certificate indicating that I had become a Fellow of the Society of Actuaries.

I had finally earned the letters "FSA" and could officially add them to my signature. I was an actuary, with the letters to prove it.

So, what has happened in the years since then?

A lot. I enjoyed a long actuarial career in which I continued to grow, contribute, and succeed. I held tightly to the letters after my name and the challenges and achievements they represented. I enjoyed connecting myself to that identity.

It was a quick and easy way for colleagues, clients, and others to understand what they could entrust me with, what value I could add, and conveyed a certain level of respect. It was a shortcut in place of offering my resumé every time I met someone new at work.

My career began shifting at some point. I was spending more time outside of the traditional actuarial realm. I was coaching and mentoring as well as leading technical projects. I was becoming more engaged in new areas.

I even held on to the letters for a while after I stopped actively working as an actuary. While the letters let potential clients know what my background was, they had very little to do with the value I could bring as a coach and speaker. They began to represent a tie to the old me. So eventually, I let them go.

If you ask me today what I do, I still start the sentence with I am. I will tell you that I am a coach and I am a speaker. I will tell you that I am an ally to actuaries and other individuals who lead with their analytical minds. But I don't need the FSA after my name anymore.

Giving up what I thought was my identity did not take away all that had come with it. It freed me up to become more true to today's self.

Our Identities

Our identity comes from how we think about ourselves. It may be tied to a title that we arrived at through years of hard work. Or it might be one that we picked up along the way with no special effort. In any case, they can become a significant part of our identity.

Of course, it is not only our careers that offer us an identity. Although those are often the first ones that we think of.

We have many dimensions to our identities which come from different areas of our lives - social, familial, and work. The various identities come and go throughout different seasons of our lives. Besides your career, perhaps you are a parent or a spouse. Maybe you are a beekeeper or an open mic star on Saturday nights.

Each of your identities defines a unique dimension of who you are. And the labels you use for them are shortcuts for people to understand you.

The challenge comes when we allow the identity to limit our activities, constrain our futures, or put an undue burden on us.

Our identities can be incredible motivators. There is a social psychological theory called identity-based motivation. It explains that in many situations, our identities or self-concepts motivate our actions and behaviors.

When we believe that an action is consistent with the identity we hold, it is much more likely that we will take that action. On the other hand, when a behavior is deemed to be inconsistent with our identity, we are less likely to engage in that behavior.

Where identities can embolden you, they can also imprison you.

At the beginning of every year, one of the most popular new year's resolutions is to lose weight. Even with all the prevailing guidance around goal setting and habit forming, most of us are doomed to failure. The donut will defeat even the best specific, measurable, actionable, relevant, and time-based goals.

We can have much better results when we tap into the power of our identity. Rather than set a specific nutritional and exercise goal, we can intentionally elevate our identity as healthy people. Since we can easily agree that a healthy person does not eat four donuts on their way to the gym, we will have an easier time driving past the donut shop.

One of the best ways to create change in your life is to focus on the positive identities you want to be associated with.

The Trap

So how does a beneficial thing such as an identity become a trap?

The same power that can keep you from getting the donuts on the way to the gym can keep you from stepping outside your comfort zone, worried about what might happen if you behave in a way inconsistent with that identity, and uncertain about your abilities to try new things.

Where identities can embolden you, they can also imprison you. Especially when the identity is superficial and temporary, or when the identity is narrow and comes with an assumed set of limiting characteristics.

The first few times I had to write a report or draft an article for work, I could hear the voice in my head reminding me that actuaries are numbers people. Not word people. What was I thinking trying to compile a coherent sentence for the broader public to see? But put me in front of a new data tool, and I would jump right in.

Our identities ... are in a constant state of evolution.

There is nothing inherently wrong with connecting ourselves with an identity. So please, do introduce yourself as doctor so-and-so if you have worked hard to get there. In fact, that can help cement your sense of accomplishment and confidence.

But also know that there are times when our identities may become obsolete, or when we have evolved into something broader. The goal is not to reduce the value in our identities. Rather, we can strive to recognize that our identities are dynamic and optional. We can at any time choose which ones we want to embrace. And we can allow them to change as we, ourselves, change.

Reconsidering Identities

It can help to think in waves. Our careers, our families, and our social structures have cycles. There are periods when we are sowing the seeds that will create our futures. We put in time and energy in order to earn specific titles, certifications, and knowledge. We nurture the skills, talents, and strengths that can bring us success in that role. And at some point, we hopefully see the fruits of our labor. We can finally reap the benefits of all of that hard work - the credibility, respect, prestige, and the career of our dreams.

However, reaping is not the end goal. At some point, that season's harvest is complete and it is time to look ahead to the next season. There comes a time to sow new seeds and nurture them to grow. They may become a new variety of what we have already grown, or they may be seeds of something entirely new.

When we miss the wave, we can remain connected to something that is further and further in the past. We become the person that says I used to be a football star. Or I used to be the CEO. Even though the wave has passed, we feel lost without the identity. We especially like to hold on to the identities that remind us of the peaks of our past.

Our identities change with each wave. They are in a constant state of evolution.

Whether from our careers or our day-to-day lives, our identities, especially those connected with a role or title, come with expiration dates. We are not meant to hold onto who we are today and let that be how we define ourselves for the rest of our lives.

There may come a time when your children are out of the house and leading their own lives, relying on you as a parent much less. Or you may reach a point where you are not getting joy and fulfillment from standing on stage at the Saturday night open mic night.

Our identities can come with inherent limitations through the stereotypes associated with them. We have a predetermined understanding of what a "typical" identity is like. Especially when we highlight one identity, we can easily succumb to these limitations.

Analytical individuals are not creative. Artists are bad at math. The stereotypes of the identity draw lines that we find difficult to cross.

We are not the only ones that connect with our identities. Everyone around us has gotten to know us through the lens of at least one of our identities. We may feel the weight of their expectations as another layer in the identity trap.

Our connections with others are often built on these identities. We have become part of a group, whether formal or informal, through our identities. Especially the identities that are expressed as our professions or our titles. Even the university from which we received our degrees can create an identity that will connect us with others.

The expectations that are set through these connections to our identity can at times become limiting. To be a part of the group, we may feel we should continue to behave as others in that group do. We may not want to rock the boat and look different.

The good news is that we have a lot of control over our identities. And we can have more than one identity. They are like puzzle pieces that we can fit together to create a more interesting and nuanced view of ourselves. We can decide whether to tie them to our titles or to the inner qualities of the person we want to be known as. The more frequently we include identities that reflect our core values and are less tied to our external accomplishments, the more stability and flexibility we discover.

When we decide to rearrange our puzzle pieces to create something new, we are not always discarding the pieces. We find new ways to fit them together that reflect who we are today. We get to enjoy more freedom in how we can express them in different areas of our lives.

Let your core values – such as kindness or adventure – become part of the identities you define. You can start identifying as a kind person or an adventurous person. You can even choose to identify as an accomplished person if creating career success is a core value.

Now consider some of the identity traps we've discussed. When you view yourself as an adventurous individual, you will have fewer hesitations about trying something new, even when it is far-flung from your current title. When you see yourself as accomplished, you may more easily find the confidence to step outside of your comfort zone.

Identities are extremely important in creating our perception of ourselves and in helping others to see quickly and clearly who we are. The most important part of our identities is their variety and flexibility, which we do have some control over.

Analyze This...

1. What one word would you use to describe yourself? Why?

2. What parts of your current identity bring you the most joy? And which parts are limiting you?

3. How might you incorporate your passions and core values into your identity? What would have to change in the way you currently identify yourself?

4. If you put up a personal billboard, what would it say? Why did you choose that message?

5. Is the identity you are holding on to helping you to grow and connect with the people that are most important right now?

SECTION 3:
PROBLEM OF UNSUSTAINABILITY

It is time to destroy the idea that we have to be constantly working and grinding in order to be successful. We have seen how easily this can put us at risk of burning out, checking out, or worrying about being found out. And it is not sustainable in the long run. Nor is it any fun.

It is also time to release ourselves from the many traps that we are getting caught in. These traps are slowing us down and making it harder to create fulfilling and sustainable lives.

If there is one undercurrent that flows through what we have talked about so far, it is that we are finding ourselves in unsustainable situations. The systems we operate in are showing signs of wear.

For much of my life, I have enjoyed living in communities that were very close to nature. It didn't take more than a 15-minute drive to get into the mountains, hike next to a stream, or bike along country roads. I used to live close enough to Yellowstone National Park to enjoy a day outing and a picnic lunch.

Our national parks and preserved spaces are wonderful reminders of the beauty and power of nature. And they rely on a similar foundation of sustainability as we do. To make them available to future generations and maintain the strength of the natural ecosystems today, we have to manage them wisely. They will not only thrive today but for the long haul if we are good stewards of the whole system.

Sustainability is the goal. Those caring for these spaces strive to create a system in which all elements can thrive with little direct intervention.

Nature, for me, has become a wonderful reminder and example of what we can create for ourselves. We each are operating in our own unique and complex system.

We coexist with everything around us - the people, the animals, the plants - as part of a complex ecosystem. And in our lives, our careers coexist with our social relationships and our communities, and with everyone around us. We operate in a complex and constantly changing system. And we, as stewards of our own lives, can choose to use our influence and control to make it a sustainable system in which we can thrive.

During the time I lived in Wyoming, I was able to witness the reintroduction of wolves to Yellowstone. It had been almost 70 years since the last wild wolf had roamed that region. We were bringing an apex predator back into an area it had once called home. It was a big deal. Environmentalists were busy with their studies.

Wolves were being reintroduced in part because there were signs of unsustainability in the park. The number of elk had been increasing, despite population mitigation efforts. Vegetation was dwindling along rivers due to overgrazing. Trees were not growing as tall as they used to.

Many scientists had theories on how the reintroduction might impact the various animal populations - from the elk and bison to the coyotes and rabbits. The hope was that the wolves would help return the elk population to a sustainable level.

In a study that was done decades later, it was fascinating to see the unexpected changes that happened after the reintroduction. Yes, elk populations reduced in number and also became healthier overall, as intended. In addition, the number of beavers and river otters grew. Vegetation returned to many riverbanks and trees began to grow taller. Many songbirds returned. Even the flow of rivers changed. The list of repercussions was long.

Not a single expert predicted every way in which the environment would be impacted by the reintroduction of wolves. This was a grand-scale experiment that seems to have moved the park's environment back toward sustainability.

There are many lessons that I have found in reflecting on this story. Three stand out for their relevance. Creating sustainability in our lives, and our careers, requires paying attention to some of these key elements of a sustainable system.

First, when we start to see signs of unsustainability, we have the choice to take action. Due to the complex nature of the system, we may not know exactly how it will turn out. But that doesn't mean we should not take action. We can approach it as an experiment. We clearly cannot manage a complex system without recognizing that the separate parts are not independent; they are interconnected.

Secondly, there are many parts to a system - whether the broad ecosystems around us or the systems of our lives, careers, and communities in which we operate daily. None of the elements in our lives exists in isolation. What happens in one area can nurture or drain other areas. We must pay attention to the resources that are available along the path and how they are both created and expended.

Finally, sustainability is not found in a future destination, but in daily practice. It requires us to shift our focus from the endpoint to our daily actions and decisions. Sustainability is created along the journey. It is in the process itself.

CHAPTER 7:
WHOLENESS

What we choose for a career and how we choose to spend our free time and build enriching relationships are all part of creating a whole life. The parts are not meant to be separated or managed independently.

The problems that we explored in the first part of the book have highlighted some of the challenges that arise when we have not created a sustainable system that considers how wellness in one area of our lives will impact our wellness in other areas.

We have sectioned off our lives and our careers and siloed our relationships. Yet there is one thing that weaves itself through each of these elements and ties them all together. That is ourselves. Our dreams. Our values. Our strengths. Our personalities.

At the busiest points in my life, during which I was working full-time in a challenging technical career as an actuary, raising young children, and trying my best to maintain meaningful relationships with family and friends, life felt full. There were many activities that filled my days… and nights… and weekends.

I had a constantly running to-do list in my head. I could tell you exactly how I was moving ahead in each role I was in, whether it was a project at work, school commitments, or my physical health.

To simplify such a complex system, I had drawn deliberate lines to disentangle the pieces. It was the analyst's approach. Create a simplified model in which each element coexists independently and separately from the others as much as possible.

Without realizing it, I was living my life in silos. Aree the actuary was kept separate from Aree the mother, the wife, or the tennis player. Each persona had its own set of rules governing how I showed up. At work, I dealt with, discussed, and focused on the challenges related to work. At home, I dealt with, discussed, and focused on the challenges at home. When I ran into a setback or disappointment at work, I would box up those emotions and leave them at work while I carried on my duties at home. When the kids had a challenging morning, I would set that aside so I could show up at work without missing a beat.

Simple meant separate. I was not paying attention to the fact that those false boundaries were actually creating more work for me. It takes a lot of energy to manage and constrain emotions.

While my life was full, my focus on the separate components of my life left me feeling less whole.

Dimensions of Wellbeing

Gallup conducted decades-long global studies of well-being, looking for elements that crossed culture and geography. Five universal elements of well-being were ultimately identified. Each element represents an area of wellness that we can influence in our lives. The choices we make create wellness in each area.

The five areas are our career, social connections, communities in which we live, finances, and physical wellness. As I consider these elements, I see how they line up with the silos that I had created.

We are the ones creating the boundaries between career and home. Between play and work. Between one identity and the next.

The elements are not isolated, though. When we improve our physical wellness, we have more energy to put into our jobs and our relationships. When we feel fulfilled in our careers, we can see the impact on our relationships and our financial wellness. It is easy to see the positive impact as it flows across the elements.

When we start to recognize each of these as parts of one whole, we give ourselves more opportunities to create the lives we want. We use the energy we create playing with our children in the evenings to carry us through a tough meeting the next morning at work. We ride the feeling of accomplishment from landing an exciting client when we are woodworking in our garage for fun on the weekend.

We have many parts of our story happening at the same time.

And then we can start to share some of our frustrations about raising kids with other parents in the workplace. This might result in new ideas for navigating parenting challenges as well as connect us with our colleagues on a new level.

Without the boundaries in place, we can let the systems interact and support each other. We can begin the difficult task of making life sustainable and fulfilling as a whole.

Harmony between elements

I have always loved music. But it wasn't until I sat through my daughters' piano lessons that I started paying attention to the different parts of classical pieces. There is always a melody, and sometimes two. While the melody takes the front stage, the other notes are supporting it and adding layers of interest. In some pieces, the melody moves from hand to hand.

In a more complex orchestra, the same nuance is at play. The melody is not always carried by one instrument or one section. It bounces around from the brass to the woodwinds to the percussion and back. It is that movement that brings depth and vibrancy to the music.

The same is true in our lives. We don't have just one storyline being told through one voice. We have many parts of our story happening at the same time.

What is the purpose of the other instruments in the orchestra when the melody is being carried in another area? Do they sit quietly and wait for their turn to play? Absolutely not. They are joining along the journey and harmonizing with the melody. They are adding interest and energy to the piece.

It's in this sense that I love the term harmony as opposed to balance for what we're trying to achieve in our life. With harmony, we can enjoy the wholeness of the music. We get to enjoy the moments when the excitement is coming from one area, while the other areas are in a support role.

Harmony. Not balance.

Wholeness. Not siloes.

I had been living my life trying to balance each separate part. My attention was divided. My storyline was divided. My energy was divided.

Sustainability requires wholeness and harmony.

Analyze This...

1. Consider the five dimensions of wellbeing. What additional areas might you add that are important in your life?

2. Which aspects of your life do you tend to keep separate, and how might they actually be interconnected?

3. How do you show up differently in each area of your life?

4. If you had a year off from work with no responsibilities or obligations, how would you spend your time?

CHAPTER 8:
RESOURCES

In creating a sustainable life, we are looking for lasting performance, well-being, and fulfillment, in which we can weather the inevitable ups and downs. To create sustainability, we must pay attention to how we both generate and consume our resources.

We have seen how burnout, whether physical, mental, or emotional, can happen when we deplete our reserves of physical, mental, and emotional energy. Every activity we participate in and every relationship we engage in require some consumption of one or more of these energies.

Of course, we could decide to live a life in which we do nothing and have no relationships. In this case, we might be able to get by without paying attention to our energy. I don't know about you, but a life without activity and relationships sounds rather boring.

Energy

We are humans, not machines. We do not plug into a consistent and constant source of energy. We are not meant to run at maximum speed for long periods.

There are hidden drains and sources we must become aware of if we want to manage our energy better.

We are at our best when we move rhythmically between spending and renewing energy. It is through this cycle that we can create sustainability.

As we've seen in the challenges of burnout, it is possible to burn out in many ways. The energy required to support ourselves in each of these aspects is a resource.

When we recognize where we have the ability to create energy and can identify what is putting the most demands on our energy in each of these areas, we can move toward a more sustainable state.

Especially in a complex system like the ones we inhabit, there are numerous ways to both create and consume energy. It is up to each of us to identify the most reliable sources of our own energy and methods to monitor and manage its consumption.

We know that healthy eating and an appropriate level of exercise can give us physical energy and stamina. We know that spending many hours at work solving challenging problems might drain both our mental and physical energies. And we know that a death in the family can take a huge toll on our emotional resources.

What interests me most are the overlooked aspects of our energy. There are hidden drains and sources we must become aware of if we want to manage our energy better. There is nothing worse than death by a thousand paper cuts.

Especially as analytical individuals, we use our brains a lot throughout the day. And that can be very taxing. The conscious problem-solving that we do is not the only place that our brains are putting in effort.

Roy Baumeister is a social psychologist who was with Case Western Reserve University in the mid-1990s. He designed an experiment involving cookies and cognition - a man after my own heart.

In his work, he had a number of adults take part in a multi-step experiment in which participants had to complete cognitive challenges. Between sessions, he brought them into a room in which there were freshly baked cookies on a table. He told one group that they could eat the cookies while waiting for the next part of the experiment. The other group was not allowed to eat them, although they could see and smell them. If they were hungry, they were given a radish.

The interesting part of the experiment came when they tested the individual's ability to solve a challenging mental problem. Those who had been allowed to freely eat the cookies were more persistent in their attempts both in number and duration when solving the problems. The group which had to refrain from eating the cookies gave up much faster.

His conclusion was not that fresh cookies are a mental superfood. Sorry.

The point is that our mental energies get depleted even when we do not realize that we are using them. Even the most mundane decisions to act or not act a certain way expend our energy.

Every decision we make takes a toll on our mental energy. And when we are making tens of thousands of decisions each day, that can have a big impact.

This is just one example of hidden drains on mental energy.

Offsetting energy drains

On the positive side, there are ways to offset some of the hidden drains.

Take the above study. It is assumed that the desire to eat the cookies is fairly consistent for every individual. But we know that each of us is very unique. If there were a vegan in the group, and they adhered very consistently to their vegan practice because it aligned with their core values, the cookies may not have posed any temptation at all. Or perhaps an individual that was very conscious of their health and followed a very strict diet. Assuming cookies were not on their diet, they may have had less of an impact on their cognitive functioning.

The less effort needed to decide whether to do something, when to do it, and how to do it, the more resources we will have available for actually doing other activities. We can look for ways to reduce the distractions and decisions that pull our energy away drop by drop.

When we are feeling the effects of any type of burnout, we can look for not only the most prominent sources and drains of our energy but the hidden ones as well.

Analyze This...

1. If you mapped your energy flow, where do you tend to create most of your energy, and where does it get used? How do these differ for your physical, mental, and emotional energies?

2. What is one thing that you could start doing today that would increase the energy available to you?

3. If you were to consider time as a resource, would you consider it as a well-managed or poorly managed resource in your current situation?

4. What boundaries might you set up to reduce the impact of some of the more significant drains on your energy or time?

CHAPTER 9:
JOURNEY FOCUS

When wolves were reintroduced to Yellowstone, it was a highly debated decision with many voices from every perspective sharing their thoughts. Of course, with any decision such as this, everyone was trying to determine what the ultimate impact would be. How would the decision turn out?

The goal was to restore a more sustainable situation in the park. It was not going to be an immediate change. Only a small number of wolves were introduced at first. One pack set loose to make their way into an environment where their ancestors used to roam.

There is an ongoing nature to sustainability.

The system did change. A different composition of flora and fauna was created. The new system is more diverse, more vibrant, and more sustainable.

The end goal of returning wolves to Yellowstone was not to change the path of a river or to re-introduce other species. It was one step in the journey of managing an ecosystem, and resetting the park on a path that could maintain the health of all that inhabit it, plants and animals alike.

Those making the decisions could not say with certainty where the decision would take the park. The same lack of predictability is at work in our own life and career. We are not targeting a destination far in the future, but striving to create a system that is healthy throughout and can sustain itself for the long run. For that reason, it is the journey that we should focus on.

Sustainability and Success

According to Merriam-Webster, when something is sustainable, it is "able to be used without being completely used up or destroyed," and "able to last or continue for a long time."

Both of these definitions suggest that sustainability is part of a process. There is an ongoing nature to sustainability. It is measured every day, not at the end of the process.

Sustainability in our lives is found in the way every part of our system interacts. The most sustainable systems are fluid and adaptable. They recognize the way our energy flows from one part of our lives to the other. In a constantly shifting environment, what makes the system sustainable is the ability to adapt and meet the needs as they evolve.

The standard definition of success is achievement-based. We measure success when we arrive at the destination. Did we meet the goal or not?

There is often a lot of space between where we are today and where we may find the end goal. We can get so focused on achieving the result that we stop paying attention to the path.

Caroline had jumped wholeheartedly into the telecommunication industry as an accountant. She was an ambitious and hard-working twenty-something and had dreams of making an impact. As she learned more about the industry in which she worked, she soon made it her goal to become the chief finance officer. She believed she could best achieve her goal of making material changes to the way that we connect with each other as a senior executive in the company.

With that end goal in mind, she arranged every part of her career to align with that goal. She watched others in leadership roles and honed the skills that would help her climb the ladder. In less than a decade, she became the first female chief finance officer the company had ever had and was handed the keys to a new office.

Sitting at the new desk, she expected to feel different. She had worked so hard to get to this exact spot. There were years of dedicated learning and chasing promotions, leading ever-growing teams, and producing financial results that confirmed her ability to grow the company.

Surprisingly, she found that she not only disliked the new role - the one that she had chased with a singular focus for years - but she also disliked who she had become. Her achievement felt hollow. She left the role and the company within a year.

What Caroline had not paid attention to in her pursuit of that one specific goal was what was happening along the journey. As she looked back to understand what had gone wrong along the way, she saw many signs that she had missed – or ignored – warning her about the unsustainability of her path. She was slowly changing how she related to her team members, shifting from a cooperative team player to an autocratic leader that had all the answers. Even though she loved exploring creative, out-of-the-box thinking, she had allowed herself to set that aside in order to become who she thought she had to be to climb the corporate ladder.

But the road TO happiness is not the road OF happiness

Many things happen between the time that we start out on a mission and when we reach our destination. Every single experience we have along the way changes us in some small or large way. With each step, we gain a new perspective of where we are, what's around us, and where we are headed.

When we are too focused on the destination, we may not be looking around enough to see what price we are paying to stay on this specific path. Our main focus is on getting to the destination as quickly as we can.

The Road to Sustainability

We are at risk of letting the ends justify the means. When we follow a sustainable path, the means are the focus, and we get to enjoy many little good-fit ends on the way.

Lucky for Caroline, when she found herself cringing at what she saw had happened along her own path, she made a change. In her next role at a new company, she kept a close eye on her authenticity and defined her success by how she was showing up every day. The next time she sat under the title of CFO, it was on her terms.

She thought she was on the road to happiness as she pursued her goal. She was convinced that once she got there, the happiness she sought would be waiting along with her new title.

But the road TO happiness is not the road OF happiness. Only one of them creates a sustainable path.

The road to happiness is focused on the destination. The happiness at the end of the path is the distant reward that is keeping you on the path.

The road of happiness creates joy along the way. Fulfillment and happiness are in the stones that line the path. You do not have to wait until the end or reach a specific destination in order to enjoy joy and fulfillment.

Which path would you rather be on?

Too often we have tied ourselves to a definition of success that is focused on the end goals.

We set our sights on what we want to achieve next. The next promotion. The next completed project. The next successful bake sale for the second-grade class. The next summited mountain.

And then we set up our days to move us closer to that end destination. We look up periodically to gauge our progress toward the goal.

But we do not look around to enjoy where we are today. We may not celebrate the little wins along the way. We don't take in the amazing views as they come. And we aren't paying attention to what is changing in us as a result of the path that we chose.

When we get to the end, we pat ourselves on the back and head off in search of the next achievement or success. This is repeatable, yes. But it is far from sustainable.

In fact, chasing achievement after achievement is a hallmark symptom of the success trap. We jump from one to the next without paying attention to what we are experiencing along the way. Our sole focus is on getting to the next achievement so we can add one more success to our list of accomplishments.

Sustainability can only be found in the process. In the journey. Creating sustainable success means paying less attention to the endpoint and spending more time in the here and now.

Analyze This…

1. Does your current definition of success relate to the end result or the experience day to day? How might you refine your definition of success to put more emphasis on the journey?

2. What method of celebrating could you experiment with to recognize progress and success along the journey?

3. If you could fast-forward to the achievement at the end of your current path, would you? Why or why not?

4. How are you different than you were five years ago?

PART 2:
CREATING SUSTAINABILITY

When I look back on my path to date, there have been times when I have been sitting out of my own life. I have turned on autopilot in a last-ditch effort to fight the feelings of burnout, end up checking out, and then worry about being found out. And I have felt the trappings of the constant search for a right answer, feeling stuck in my past success, and being tied to my limiting identities.

I also thought that these were just part of the process. If we are going to be successful, it is going to take hard work. Hard work means struggles. Since each of these is a struggle in its own right, they were a sign that I was doing it right, right?

Unfortunately, the answer is a resounding no. There are indeed struggles on the path, even when it is sustainable. When we are living sustainably, though, we are equipped with the energy, time, and tools to manage through the struggles without ending up suffering on the other side. What I was taking as a sign that I was working hard was in fact a sign that what I was doing was hardly working.

A lot of the challenges I faced were because I did not recognize how my system worked. I was focused on managing each independent part. I could not see what the whole of me had become and how the different dimensions of myself interacted with each other.

I certainly wasn't keeping an eye on my physical, mental, and emotional energies. It was much easier to put things on autopilot and hope that would save what little energy I had left.

Luckily there came a time when I finally learned to step out on my own and start navigating intentionally. I was able to create the sustainability that I had long been missing.

Maybe you saw yourself in one of the elements in the first part of this book. Maybe, like me, you saw yourself in all of them.

It is time to turn our attention to the puzzle pieces that you can use to build a sustainable life for yourself. The remainder of the book is focused on setting yourself up to step out into your own sustainable life. A life that keeps you energized, engaged, and thriving.

The path of sustainability is one you can create for yourself daily. It starts with knowing who you are and what is integral to your system. It is in how you want to show up in your community and your relationships. It integrates all the aspects of your life. Once you know who you are and how you can live authentically, you can show up consistent with those truths, and connect honestly with others.

As we learned earlier in looking at Yellowstone, no system as complex as our lives is static. There are continuously moving parts. No one action will set us up for the future of our dreams. Any action we take today will cascade changes through the system. We are creating a different future for ourselves every day. And we have the tools to navigate that new future.

The world in which we operate is constantly changing and moving. We are dynamic and evolving. And that is why navigating and influencing the sustainability of such a dynamic and complex system requires continual motion in the choices we make each day.

There are three elements that will help you step out and create a sustainable life.

The first is in recognizing the wholeness of who you are and how you are showing up. When we close the gap between what we know of ourselves on the inside and what we show externally, we are honoring ourselves. Much of this falls into the realm of authenticity. We can learn the art of authenticity and use it in our careers and outside of them to make it easier for us to show up as ourselves.

The second element is that of taking back the control of our life. We have to be willing to turn off the autopilot. As you move into sustainability, you are moving forward intentionally. That means that you get to choose something hard you want to do. There is likely not a single person among us that wants to sit back and coast through life. We want challenges, and when we choose some of those challenges, we can face them more effectively. When making choices, we recognize that there is no right answer. The best way to do that is to look at your motions, your actions, and your decisions as experiments.

It wouldn't be realistic to think that we are operating in a vacuum. While we do get to choose and experiment, we do not know how things will turn out. We are operating in cultures within our companies and our communities that influence the world in which we operate.

There are many ways our brains can help us create the sustainable lives we desire. The first way we can use our brains, especially for those of us that are analytically inclined, is by identifying patterns. Through the experimenting we do as we move through our careers and our lives, we're gathering data. We're paying attention to what works, what feels good, and what doesn't work. We're asking questions. All of this offers us data in which we can start looking for patterns.

Sustainability comes more easily with the proper motivation. So many of our challenges in the first part were created through or as a side effect of extrinsic motivators. Choosing the best way to motivate ourselves can help us create the energy cycle that sustainability requires.

Our brains are amazing tools. Even though I give them some of the blame for getting us into this mess, they play a big role in keeping us in a sustainable life. They are our friends in the end, and we can help them do what comes naturally and set them up for success by taking care of them.

SECTION 4:
ART OF AUTHENTICITY

Authenticity requires the alignment of the head, heart, mouth, and feet. When we connect what is true in our thoughts, feelings, words, and actions, we can not only be more certain about our footing on a journey, but those that are following us can trust where they are headed as well.

In the spirit of authenticity, I will admit something to you now: I am not a shoe person. I don't like shopping for them. I often don't like wearing them… unless they are my well-worn Birkenstocks. And I don't spend a lot of time thinking about them.

I am very practical with my shoes. I buy them when I need them, which translates to many months after the prior pair that served the same purpose have worn out. I have one pair of black dress shoes in my closet.

This trait nearly stopped me from saying yes to something I wanted to do recently. I had just met Angie, a dynamic woman with big dreams and a knack for getting interesting people in a room together. She was going to be organizing a local women's networking event. From our conversation, I knew I wanted to be a part of it. So, when she closed with, "Oh, and wear your boldest shoes! The theme is Women Who Stand Out!" I could feel my heart sink.

My mind immediately brought up pictures of bright red, high-heeled, stiletto shoes. Not only unlike anything I have in my closet but also the kind of shoes that would put me in the hospital after two steps. Nothing about the pictures that I conjured up brought any sense of confidence, ease, or comfort. Quite the opposite.

As an introvert, networking events already put me out of my comfort zone. The last thing I would need is to also be hobbled physically.

I was facing an authenticity challenge. There was no way I would be able to feel like myself if I showed up wearing the bold shoes in my head.

I almost blurted out "I'm sorry…did you say September 8? I forgot about this other thing I have that day… all day… and night. Good luck to you and your bold shoes."

Instead, I resolved two things at that moment. First, I will be going to the event. And second, I will wear my version of bold shoes. Shoes that exude me-ness. Shoes in which I can feel confident, comfortable, and safe, as well as bold.

There is no reason that I can't stand out in a crowd while still being myself. In fact, as I thought about it, that might make it easier to stand out. I am my own person. I could be the only person in the room not wearing bright red stiletto heels.

Brené Brown said it well… "Authenticity is the daily practice of letting go of who we think we're supposed to be and embracing who we are." Even when we are embracing only our shoes.

What does a pair of shoes have to do with our authenticity?

They are an example of recognizing what is true about you. It is about understanding your system.

My challenge above was not that I didn't want to be bold. I did.

I chose to take it as a challenge. I prepared myself to do things I was neither good at nor enjoyed, knowing that once I got through that point, I could return to being me.

Interestingly enough, I found a funky pair of Vans that fit the bill. They looked like no shoes I had ever seen anyone else wear. They had a mix of checker-board backgrounds, flowers, the earth, and inspirational sayings. They were eclectic and natural, comfortable, and carried a message. They spoke to me.

The most interesting thing about the shoes is not how they made me feel at the networking event, but what has happened since. Every time that I wear the shoes, people comment on them, start a conversation, and engage. That was not the intent. Like the wolves in Yellowstone, taking one small step toward my authenticity changed many things around me in ways that I could not anticipate.

It all started with recognizing my truth and deciding to walk boldly into it.

It is this type of authenticity - considering what about the external expectations (whether true or not) do not align with who we are and then figuring out our truth - that opens the doors to sustainability.

It is a deliberate move away from historical career advice of 'find someone who is successful and do what they did.' I get it… it can be tempting to take someone's playbook. It worked for them, didn't it? When their playbook doesn't fit with your reality, though, it is a recipe for disaster. Following it and expecting it to lead you to the same success will not work. There is one key ingredient that is not the same. You.

Why is authenticity so important? Living inauthentically is living a lie. As Lana Winters says, "Lies are like scars to the soul. They destroy you."

Especially when the lies are about who we are - our core values, natural strengths, and personality - those scars sit deep.

There is no one way to live authentically. Your authenticity and how you choose to express it will look different than anyone else's because you are different from everyone else. It's up to you how you put yourself forward and the parts of you that you share.

Through my own experience in striving to show up authentically as well as helping others to do the same, I have found that there is an art to it. There are three core elements that, when put together, can set the stage for sustainability. Conveniently, they conform to the acronym A-R-T. Aligned - Relevant - Tact-y.

It starts with being aligned with who you are in this moment, as you develop an awareness of what makes you unique, what is happening around you and in you today, and understand how this differs from what you show externally. Once you recognize your alignment, you get to choose the most relevant parts to share in each situation. The way you share your truths will require enough tact to be effective, but not so much that it holds you back.

CHAPTER 10:
ALIGNED

Recall the challenge I had trying to rainmake using someone else's playbook. A few years later, at a new company, I was again in a rainmaking role. This time, I approached it from my strengths. I leaned into my ability to collaborate with colleagues and layer my expertise onto theirs to offer broader support to clients. The reason this approach worked so much better for me was because it aligned with my truths. Rather than pick up someone else's playbook, I was able to structure my actions around who I was and what came naturally.

I have always felt a need to be comfortable and confident in a topic before I can effectively share that idea with someone else. I work best collaboratively, and not in direct competition. And I need to connect on a personal level with those I work with whether they are clients or colleagues.

Once I knew the endpoint - bringing in clients - and had the freedom to find my own way, I could create my own playbook. One in which I could build my plays around my values and strengths.

Through these different rainmaking approaches, I noticed a few distinct outcomes. First, when I was able to stay consistent with my values and leverage my strengths, I still had plenty of energy to focus on the rest of my projects that were unrelated to rainmaking. When I was not aligned, I was so drained from my rainmaking efforts that I could not focus well anywhere else.

Second, I was much more successful using my own plays. I am sure potential clients could sense my hesitations and lack of confidence in the cold calls. I probably sounded like a computer-generated voice that was reading a script I was not emotionally attached to. Afterall, that is essentially what I was – a voice following a program.

When I wasn't showing up authentically it was hurting me.

Being aligned with our values is a choice.

Adrienne is an accomplished actuary. She grew her career at a national consulting firm. She was quickly recognized as a high performer and asked to take on growing responsibilities each year. She rose quickly through the ranks and made many allies along the way. Much of the work she was involved in played to her strengths - as a technical actuary and as a team player.

Through her ascent, she paid attention. She looked ahead to the roles above her, knowing that she was headed for those seats if she wanted them. The higher she rose, the less she liked what she was seeing. It began to look like a cutthroat game to get ahead to the next levels. The team collaboration was dwindling. Everyone was out for themselves.

When she brought it up to her manager, a friend and trusted advisor, he confirmed her view. The company culture was strong. The pressure to grow the business was high, and it seemed that certain behaviors were not only condoned but expected at the next level. If she were to advance beyond this point, she would be asked to violate some of her personal values.

Eventually, she had to make a decision. She had been very successful to this point. Her experience was positive, and she loved what she was doing. She could decide to stay where she was, working for someone that she trusted and liked working for, who could buffer some of the value conflicts she was feeling. But that would mean giving up on becoming the leader she knew she wanted to be.

When she envisioned who she would have to become in order to "succeed" at the next level, she thought long and hard. She knew that the values of the company did not align with her core values. She could decide to stay and take on the system.

Rather than stay and fight, or stay and not grow, she left the company. Instead of seeking out a different company with different values, she took another tack. She decided to build something from the ground up that reflected her core values. She opened her own consulting firm.

She knew that building a company from scratch is not an easy task. She would face many challenges, some of which would be outside of her strengths and skillset.

Stepping away from a comfortable and successful established career is also not an easy task. We have seen how powerful the hold of success and identity can be. She was willing to take those on, driven by the vision of what she was building. She chose a different, yet still challenging path.

Today, she heads a small and growing boutique actuarial consulting company. One in which her values can be seen and felt in every aspect from the way they operate to how they communicate to who is on the team. While it has not been easy every day, she very much prefers to fight through the challenges she chose.

She was able to build something new by leaning into her authenticity.

Authenticity

Authenticity seems like a buzzword that is being thrown about in the business world as the answer to every challenge these days. It isn't a magic bullet, but I believe it is one of the key elements to creating sustainability.

It is about showing up as yourself. It means recognizing what is true about you and allowing those elements to be a part of what you do each day. It is about choosing how you will display and embody what is true for you in all your actions and relationships.

When you drive a car, the first hint that your wheels are not aligned is that you feel resistance. Your gas mileage decreases. There is a slight shaking when you drive. If you take your hands off the wheel, you start drifting off course.

Mechanics have tools to measure to what degree each wheel is off-center. There is a measurable truth at which point all four wheels are perfectly aligned.

If only we had such a clear measurement of truth for our lives that we can align to.

The rumblings and friction we feel in burnout and in the traps we find ourselves in are hints that we are not properly aligned. We check out when we sense that something is off, even when we cannot put our finger on it. We already know when we are not properly aligned.

What are we aligning with? What are we supposed to be authentic to?

To push the car analogy a little farther, there are parts of the car you can easily alter. You can change the paint or add a hitch to pull a trailer. You could even overhaul the engine to make it more powerful. But you cannot change the fact that the wheels need to point in the same direction in order to move forward smoothly.

It is similar to us. There are elements that we can easily change. Our skills. What we do each day. But underneath it all are the parts of us that do not change as readily - our core values, natural strengths, and personality. They are uniquely ours. These are the parts that define our alignment. We can take steps to recognize what these are for us today and how they show up in different circumstances.

Values

Core values are a defining system of beliefs that establish right and wrong for us. They are generally developed in our youth, although how we define them and the weight they have at different seasons in our life may shift. Our core values guide us as we make decisions, build relationships, and solve problems.

Our core values shape how we experience the world.

They are unique to you. Many exercises I have seen focus on choosing your core values out of a discrete list of words. Even when the whittled-down one-word core value is the same as the person next to you, you get to define it and determine how you want to embody it and bring it to life.

For example, integrity is a common core value. If you ask 10 people to define integrity, you would likely get 10 unique definitions. One might focus on consistency between their words and their actions. Another may define it as always speaking the truth.

Once you define your core values, you also get to decide how you want to see them take shape in different situations. They can define how you act, as you focus your energy on embodying the value in your actions. Or you might shift the focus to encouraging others to act with more integrity so that the world around you reflects your values.

Our core values shape how we experience the world. They dictate our response to different situations. They create the "why" behind what we do.

During the various interviews conducted for this book, I was struck by one situation in which two people had opposite reactions to the same phrase.

"It's just a job."

If someone were to say this to you, do you nod in agreement, confident that what you do in your career is only a small piece of who you are? Or do you tighten up and defend the fact that what you do is so much more than "just a job"… it is an extension of how you make an impact in the world?

Whatever your response, it is not right or wrong. It is a reflection of what you hold as your core values.

For Mark, providing for and being present with his family is one of his core values. He wants to be in a job that provides enough financial security that he can offer a good home for his growing family. He wants to have time and energy to spend with his family. While he also wants to be engaged in his work, he knows that any role that drains his emotional and physical energy can make it harder for him to show up as the father he wants to be. When he finds a job that fits this bill, he is happy. And many jobs could fit this bill.

So, when his manager pulled him aside and said, "It's just a job", it was very comforting. It helped him to realize that yes, his job is a small part of the big picture that he is creating. What's most important to him is how he can show up for his family.

On the other hand, it is important for Sandy to be able to make an impact at work. She wants to be a part of creating a welcoming and encouraging culture for everyone at her company to grow in. She chose her career carefully and said yes to the job because it would allow her to fulfill her big dreams.

When she heard those same words, "It's just a job," it took her aback. And she pushed back. She cannot bear to say it is just a job. She needs to be in a position where she is making an impact on the people that she works with and in the industry as a whole. Her core values include doing work that matters.

Four little words. "It's just a job." Two completely different alignments. Each true for the individual and the core values they hold.

Natural Strengths

Our natural strengths are defined in positive psychology as our built-in capacities for a particular way of thinking, feeling, and behaving. They are our natural tendencies for operation. They are "how" we do what we do when left to our own devices.

We don't set out to deliberately develop and create our strengths. Through our genes and our upbringing, they become ingrained in us. We don't choose our strengths... we discover them.

Some of us are very analytical (ahem... hello!). We want to see data and make decisions based on facts. That is our comfort zone, and it comes easily. Others are idea-generating machines, always thinking of new and different ways to approach a challenge. Or maybe a strength is in our ability to develop others. Everyone we come into contact with suddenly starts to grow in ways they never thought possible.

It is these strengths that allow us to move forward in whatever endeavor we choose because they transcend the activity. You may have a natural ability to stay calm in tense situations, break down a complex problem, or communicate clearly in any situation. You likely cannot name where you learned how to do that. It's been a part of you for that long.

There are many ways that you can identify your strengths. There are assessments available, such as Clifton Strengthsfinder, that will label your strengths based on your response to different situations. The people you work closest with can likely identify your strengths. They see evidence in your actions each day. When you pay attention to the compliments that you receive, especially the ones to which you initially think "that's nothing... anyone can do that." You are seeing hints at your natural strengths.

Personalities

Our personalities make up a third dimension of our alignment. They reflect our way of thinking, feeling, and behaving. They are what make up "who" we are at the core. They have been developed through our lives, shifting slowly, if at all.

Our personalities are influenced by our temperament and our experiences, and they are exhibited in how we interact with others. While there are formal assessments such as the enneagram and Myers Brigs personality profiles, what is most important in recognizing your personality in terms of alignment is that it is who you are. There is no judgment around them. You may be introverted or extroverted, calm or anxious, arrogant or generous. Maybe you are a little bit of each of these.

I am a card-carrying introvert. I am more than comfortable in quiet and solitude.

A good friend of mine, another coach and speaker who has built a thriving speaking business, is often mistaken for an extrovert based on his actions during events he speaks at.

When on stage, he can increase the energy of a room without breaking a sweat. He seems to effortlessly work the room in networking situations, bouncing from conversation to conversation. He connects with and appears to be comfortable talking to anyone he shakes hands with.

Yet when asked, he will admit "I am an introvert who has learned to do extroverted things."

The more I reflect on that phrase, the more I have come to realize how wise and accurate it is. Every one of us can learn skills outside of our personalities. We can learn how to hold a conversation when we are much more comfortable in the quiet.

Doing something outside of our comfort zone does not mean we are becoming what we are doing. By doing the things that an extrovert might do on the stage and in a networking situation, he looks like an extrovert. He is using certain skills. But he has not changed who he is.

He still needs downtime and quiet away from the crowds or a walk along a still nature trail in order to regain his energy. He honors the reality of his personality.

Cognitive Dissonance

When we are trying to live up to a persona that is not congruent with who we are, our actual personality, we will experience what psychologists call cognitive dissonance. There is an inconsistency between who we portray ourselves to be and who we are.

It can happen at work, at home, and even (or especially) on social media. Anytime we are portraying ourselves differently on the outside than we are inside, we can feel the effect of cognitive dissonance.

In his book The Presentation of Self in Everyday Life, Erving Goffman introduced the idea of our front stage and our backstage selves. The front stage self is the performative and polished persona, playing to a specific audience. The backstage self is who we are when we are not acting or filling a role. The gap between the two can be great.

Authenticity is about reducing that gap.

It can be hard to let others see our backstage when we, ourselves, are busy judging it.

Cognitive dissonance is a drain on our energy that takes precious resources away from our ability to create sustainability. It can be offset by recognizing and embracing the truth about our backstage - who we truly are. When we start to believe the front stage persona to be the truth, we are setting ourselves up on an unsustainable path.

I would add one element to my friend's quote - I am an introvert that has learned to do extroverted things while holding tight to my introverted nature.

We can honor our personalities and natural tendencies while using skills that look like the opposite. That is not contradictory. That is a skill. It is a skill that allows you flexibility in different circumstances and does not endanger your sustainability.

Our authenticity is not at risk as long as we are aware of the risk of cognitive dissonance. We can even let others in on the secret.

There is an art to showing others the backstage.

Letting others in on the backstage view can be a powerful way to strengthen relationships, build trust, and make it easier to live aligned and authentically in the long run.

It can be hard to let others see our backstage when we, ourselves, are busy judging it.

People often compliment me on being "calm and grounded." The judgmental part of my brain (the one that is often much more engaged when I turn the lens on myself) immediately converts it to "boring." Of course, my logical brain knows that this is not what they meant.

"You are so calm and grounded" is usually short for "you are so calm and grounded, and I admire that about you because it is so different from what I feel and experience in myself. How the hell do you do that?"

It is the same way that I, as an introvert, am in awe of the extrovert that can go running into a room of 100 people and come out two hours later with more energy than they started with.

Aligning with your truths means accepting and embracing who you are so you can harness the power within you.

It is in these moments that we can put on the lens of awareness and authenticity and say, "heck yeah, this IS who I am. And it serves me well."

Aligning

Recognizing your values, strengths, and personality will get you aligned with the why, the how, and the who of how you operate. There is one more aspect of alignment that cannot be ignored. That is what is happening in your world today.

Every day, we are experiencing life. Those experiences, the good and the bad, the big and the small, are also a part of how we show up authentically. None of us lives in a world with no spilled coffee and rude drivers. Nor do we live in a world of perpetual green lights and strangers at Starbucks buying us a coffee.

We are actively managing careers, families (both up and down generations), hobbies, and everything else that makes up our lives. What happens in one arena will affect how we show up elsewhere.

We can integrate those happenings and the impact they have on us and those around us into our authenticity. We don't have to pretend that the world is all rosy, nor wallow in every bad thing. But we can share those as part of our truths. We can acknowledge the impact they have on our ability to show up the way we want to in a given situation.

Being aligned has many dimensions. The common thread is aligning with the truth of today's situation.

Analyze This...

1. Get clear on your core values. Not only name them but also define them in your own words and identify how you intend to activate them.

2. Uncover your natural strengths. Consider especially activities and perspectives that come easily to you. What do you do well without even trying?

3. How might some of the qualities that you are keeping in the "backstage" area serve you in a current situation? What steps can you take to bring those to the front stage?

4. Create a personal mission statement that incorporates your core values, natural strengths, and reflects your unique personality. It can be geared toward a specific role, such as leader, or keep it general.

CHAPTER 11:
RELEVANT

Once we are clear on who we are, how we show up, and see clearly what is in our backstage area, we are poised to open the door to others. We can let them in so that they can better understand us and we can work together more effectively.

What holds us back from throwing open the door to the backstage to all who come? Fear that the magic will disappear? Fear that they won't like what is behind the curtain? Not sure when to show what parts?

All of this requires vulnerability and some intention. It feels much less risky to stick with the front stage view, with all its polish and carefully crafted and curated props, and you playing a role. Yet this approach is often a significant contributor to the traps and challenges of unsustainability.

Vulnerability

Brené Brown, an author and research professor at the University of Houston, defines vulnerability as "uncertainty, risk, and emotional exposure." None of these are typically things that analytical individuals like us eagerly run toward... until we can understand the benefits and a few ways to mitigate the risks.

While vulnerability can feel like it has a core of shame and fear, it is also the birthplace of joy, creativity, and belonging. And it is a cornerstone in the foundation of a sustainable life.

Vulnerability can strengthen the relationships that we depend on at work, at home, and throughout our community. It can happen when showing empathy, sharing information, or simply expressing what you need in the moment. It is an invitation to those around you to see you more clearly and for them to know that it is safe to do the same.

Those of us that love to solve problems may be tempted to view vulnerability as bringing new problems to the forefront. It can seem like we are adding to the complexity of an already challenging issue.

Vulnerability will allow you to be more creative in problem-solving. By putting more information on the table for consideration, we offer new paths in which to explore, grow, and learn. With a new perspective, we may just identify a solution that honors our values and utilizes our strengths as well as addresses the original challenge.

Amy C. Edmondson, a Harvard professor and researcher, has identified one consistent quality of high-performing teams. They all enjoy psychological safety. Everyone on the team is able to be open about their whole selves without fear of repercussions.

Psychological safety develops when there is mutual respect and trust for each other. Acknowledging your humanness creates a safe space for others to bring themselves forward.

While Dr. Edmondson's work has focused on teams, I believe the results can be transferred to all of our relationships. If we cannot be authentic by sharing who we truly are and what makes us tick, we are confining ourselves to the front stage. We are limiting our ability to work together and relate to each other honestly.

Relevance

So, which parts of our truth are the best to share when being authentic and vulnerable? Do we just blurt out anything and everything that passes through our conscious mind?

> *With authenticity, the goal is to connect, to be*
> *understood, and to share your perspective.*

If we were to throw open the doors to everything true about us today, at best, not a soul would have the time to sort through all of that information. At worst, we have diluted any chance of connection by causing distraction and confusion.

We can use intentional authenticity and vulnerability as a tool that allows us to embrace the whole of ourselves as we honor our core values, leverage our natural strengths, and let our personalities flow. We are sharing more of our backstage because by doing so, we are embracing a more holistic approach.

The goal of being open and authentic about your values, your strengths, and what's happening in your world today is not to manipulate the situation to evoke a certain response or outcome. With authenticity, the goal is to connect, to be understood, and to share your perspective.

We can be selective in what we choose to share without being manipulative. In different companies, in different communities, and in different situations, what we share may vary greatly. It depends on the level of psychological safety that we already enjoy. Starting small can begin to create psychological safety where none exists today.

The best rule of thumb and the second element of the ART of authenticity is to strive for relevance.

Like any shift in a system, when we are vulnerable and sharing ourselves, it is kind of like introducing a new element to an ecosystem. We cannot foresee what changes might come from it, but that does not mean that we should not be experimenting.

Rules of Thumb

There are a few rules of thumb that can help when deciding whether something is relevant and will help grow a relationship or contribute to addressing a challenge.

Relevance (if you ask mister Webster) means that something is appropriate to the current time, period, or circumstance.

Often, we can share stories of similar circumstances that we have been involved in. Or we can share a lesson that we learned through a similar challenge.

Inappropriate and irrelevant sharing can be very counterproductive. While what you are offering may be true, when the connection is not clear, those around you might start off on their own internal (and unsuccessful) quest to try to connect what you were talking about with the issue at hand. They are effectively derailed from following and contributing to the discussion.

That doesn't mean that sharing something about your experience as a rodeo clown during college doesn't have a place in the boardroom. You may just need to be prepared to explain that that is where you developed your sense of teamwork and how it applies to today's situation.

Something can be relevant because it impacts our effectiveness, focus, mindset, or emotional state. Let's face it. What is going on in one part of our world - be it work, home, or community - can impact how we show up for and with others in all of the other areas.

We are the thread that ties all the parts of our lives together. We are the one consistent element. While we bring different parts of ourselves to the forefront in each of these arenas, the energy we create when we are in our beloved woodworking station in our garage can feed our ability to put in extra effort at our day job. The emotions we experience after a particularly challenging meeting at work can follow us home.

When something is going on that is impacting your ability to show up and participate or contribute to a situation, it is relevant to share some of that situation. You don't have to include every gory detail, but offering some information allows others to understand what they are observing. Offering others some perspective into what is going on in different areas of your life can provide context for them to understand your emotional state and energy levels.

By showing up authentically and sharing both the good and the bad, and how it impacts you today, you can potentially shift a situation from one in which your team misunderstands your bad mood as a reflection of their results to one in which they can empathize with the fact that your dog left an unwelcome surprise on the carpet that morning.

Relevance may be created through the impact we can have on those around us. A great leader is able to use all sorts of tools to connect with, unite, and encourage their teams. Authenticity is one of these tools. The stories we share about ourselves may be just the thing that our teams need to hear in order to have the courage to find their path through a challenge or to unlock their creativity.

Relevance is in the eye of the beholder.

We might share experiences in which we failed or violated our values. Sometimes the hardest lessons we have learned can serve as inspiration to others. Being vulnerable about our struggles reminds others that we are also human.

Other times, we can share a funny story about ourselves or something that happened to us to lighten the mood in a room. These are all examples of authenticity building relationships and enabling us to live truer to our values and strengths.

The key is to ask yourself a few questions before jumping in (or use it as a post-mortem if you jumped in and things went south).

What is my purpose for sharing that part of me?

How might what I am about to share impact those in the room?

How might I feel after sharing this? What impact will it have on me?

Sometimes we have to put something out there and let others decide whether it is relevant. If you hear "Me, too!" or "Ah, now I understand where you are coming from and why you have the opinion you do," you're on the path to relevance. If you are met with blank stares, you might need to add a little explanation.

Relevance is situational. It is tricky. Something relevant in one situation may not be so in another. What is relevant today may be irrelevant tomorrow. It is a constantly moving target.

In the end, relevance happens at the other end of the interaction. What you put out is only relevant if someone else connects with it, understands your perspective better, or sees how their values relate to yours. Relevance is in the eye of the beholder.

We cannot accurately predict the outcome when we lean into our authenticity. We cannot control the relevance of what we share. Our responsibility, and a key step toward creating a sustainable path for ourselves, is to put a true version of ourselves out to the world. We can start there.

Analyze This...

1. Consider a current relationship that you would like to strengthen. Share one small new element about yourself with the individual that might help build a stronger bridge between you.

2. List out different aspects of your authentic self that you have identified from earlier exercises. For each, come up with a situation or two where that aspect of your authentic self might be relevant.

3. Write a letter from your future self. In it, reflect on how you have incorporated your authenticity into more areas of your life and the impact that it has had on your success and happiness. Be specific in describing how others responded to your vulnerability.

CHAPTER 12:
TACT-Y

I have seen many instances where a person will raise their flag of authenticity and charge into battle with it. They are intent on living authentically, and at the same time seemingly unconcerned with or unaware of the impact it has on others.

They look somewhat like a bull in a china shop. They barrel through relationships and situations without much regard for what may have been broken and left in the aftermath. Their authenticity is legitimate, and they are being true to themselves. But there is no attention being paid to how their authenticity is affecting the world around them.

This flamboyant approach to authenticity is a way to avoid vulnerability and responsibility. It is authenticity as armor.

At the other end of the spectrum, and one in which I have tended to reside, is authenticity that feels more like a gentle breeze in the china shop. The breeze can come in and wrap around the china, but it is not strong enough to move any of the pieces. It may feel good as it passes through, however, it does not leave any lasting impact. There is no evidence that it was there once it has passed through.

Those who wear their authenticity more as a breeze are not committing deeply to their truths. They are authentic only to the point where it is comfortable for them and others. Theirs is a powerless authenticity.

There is a place in between these approaches in which growth, impact, and connection can flourish.

In ancient China, the cracks in porcelain pieces would be filled in with gold. The cracks could then be visible and celebrated. The repairs created something that was stronger and more interesting.

I received a compliment years ago that struck me as odd at the time. "You are able to tell someone that they are being a jackass without offending them."

At first, I wasn't sure what to think of it. Was it a compliment? Was telling someone they were a jackass a good thing? Had I called this person a jackass at some point?

As I think more about that comment, I realize that it is a love child of my natural strength of harmony and my core value of integrity. When I am being authentic to those elements of myself, I will both speak the truth and maintain harmony when I do so.

It turns out this is a good example of being somewhere between a bull in a china shop and being a breeze. Without knowing it, at least in that one instance, I was what I now call tact-y.

Defining Tact-y

It is no secret around our house that I love to make up words. Just ask anyone in our family what it means when our youngest daughter gets 'dogstracted' on a walk. Part of this tendency might be due to my math brain in which words are a marvel. It is also darn fun, and it amuses me.

In talking about authenticity, we started with knowing the truths that align with you today. And we noted the importance of striving for relevant ways to show up that are consistent with your authentic self. The third principle is in how we engage our authenticity. And that is what takes tact.

We are not trying to sugarcoat our truths or walk on eggshells. Going back to the china shop, too much tact creates a breeze. Too little tact becomes a bull. Being tact-y might still do some damage. There will be chips here or a crack there when something lands too hard. The good news is that we can equip ourselves to deal with the damage authentically as well.

If we are not regularly required to have some challenging and uncomfortable conversations, it might be a sign that we are showing up more like the gentle breeze. In this case, we can explore whether we are showing enough of ourselves.

And if every conversation we have is turning into an all-out argument, we might want to check whether we are a card-carrying bull. Where can we make room for the authenticity of others in the same space?

When you are shooting to be tact-y, there will be times when things you say or do, as you are showing up authentically, do not land as you hoped they might. We do not have control over the outcome. But we do have a responsibility to address the outcome.

We can circle back and deal with the damage head-on through humility. Humility, as C.S. Lewis notes, is "not about thinking less of yourself, but thinking of yourself less." It is an opportunity to practice emotional intelligence and communication. We can stay authentic to our unique strengths and values and personalities as we do so.

Your Tact-y

What your tact-y looks like will depend on your unique set of values, strengths, and personality.

How you go about your tact-y will be as individual as you are.

As I reflect on the compliment at the beginning of the chapter, I can see how it was consistent with my values and strengths. I am all about honesty and making sure people have the information they need, even if it is something that they don't want to hear. I know I would love to have people call me out - in a tact-y way - when I am being a jackass. And I also have a knack for creating harmony. For me, being tact-y leans on harmony and integrity.

Others may come at it through humor, deep connection, adventure, or wanting to grow others. We can engage our values, strengths, and personality in both the way we walk out our authenticity as well as the way we respond to and deal with how that authenticity is received.

How you go about your tact-y will be as individual as you are.

All three of the elements of the ART of authenticity are important for putting yourself - your true self - out into the world. They are the starting point for creating your own sustainable life and career. Sustainability relies on operating in the whole truth of your system. And who you are is at the core of that system.

Our identities are not defined by what we choose to do each day. Our true identities are defined by how we show ourselves each day. They are reflections of our values, strengths, and personality. These identities unite the system in which we operate - our careers, our communities, and our social lives.

By aligning with our truths, we can reduce the energy drain that comes from pretending to be who we are not. We can see what is most important for us and our sustainability. And we can choose to intentionally act consistent with who we are today and what is happening in our world.

Once we are clear on who we are, we get to convey select elements of our truths in each unique situation. What we choose to share depends on the relevance for that circumstance. While there is some strategy in identifying which parts of our alignment are relevant to a given situation, we do not have control over how our authenticity will be received.

When we can be tact-y in showing up authentically, we can challenge ourselves to find a place between the bull and the breeze. We can be prepared to find growth in ourselves and others.

It is through appearing in the world as you truly are that you are mastering the first part of creating a sustainable life. You are being true to who you are today. You are practicing the art of you.

Analyze This...

1. Practice in a low-stakes situation. If you are holding back being more outgoing at work because you are afraid you will be "too much", consider practicing letting that part of your personality out by being more outgoing when waiting in line at a coffee shop.

2. Consider the last instance you were either too much of a bull or too much of a breeze. Look at the characteristics of the situation and identify the triggers that likely contributed to your more extreme behavior.

3. Take an improv class. This builds not only the humor muscle, but the ability to listen to respond.

4. Ask a trusted colleague or friend to assess your tact-y-ness. Have them rate you as a bull, breeze, or somewhere in between. Consider how their assessment differs from your own perception.

SECTION 5:
INTENTIONAL NAVIGATION

Navigation is not about finding and following true north on a compass, not the compass in your heart, not the compass in your head. Navigation is about sailing a little crookedly, adjusting, and setting your course in order to create a meaningful journey.

I began intentionally navigating my career much later than I could have. There were so many other ways that were working well enough. I followed in someone else's footsteps. I took advantage of opportunities that appeared along my path. And I was enjoying a good enough career and life.

But it wasn't sustainable in the end. While it was relatively easy and brought me monetary and promotional success, eventually the path led me to a place where I could not ignore the misalignment anymore. I hadn't been paying attention to the forks in the road where I should have taken a slight turn in a new direction.

Of course, at various times, there are intentional decisions. We consider which line of study to take, the career that will offer the most money, or the one that will make our parents the proudest.

The navigation that I have found to be most sustainable is similar to what we use when we are hiking in the mountains or exploring a wilderness area. There are many paths that lead in various directions.

They criss-cross each other as they pass by waterfalls, scenic overlooks, and wildlife viewing areas. They each offer different yet incredibly amazing views and highlights.

In such an environment, we are required to constantly evaluate what we expect to find around the next corner and to make decisions about whether we want to continue on the original path or take a chance on a new one. We are watching the skies for changes in weather. We are guided more by direction than by destinations. And we find joy and sustainability in the path itself.

Intentional navigation in the wild requires three core principles to create sustainability. The first principle is that we have choices. Even when you believe there is no option, there often is. Not choosing to do something different is choosing to stay on the current path. It is through becoming aware of the choices we are unintentionally making and taking back control through intentional choices that we can influence our current situations.

The second principle is viewing our decisions as experiments. We can commit to a certain path for a period, see what we can learn, and decide whether we want to make a change at a later point. This allows us to both enjoy the experience of the experiment and pay attention to the data we collect so we have more information for future decisions.

And finally, because we are not in control of everything in our environment, we have to recognize the impact of the external environment in which we are traveling. Like weather, these can both help and hinder our ability to move effectively along the chosen paths.

Chapter 13:
CHOICE

"It's unusual to land a job that was designed for you, but it's possible to tailor a job into one that suits you." — Adam Grant.

Our oldest daughter attended a Montessori preschool. I remember many days when she would come home eager to share what she had chosen to work on that day. Her whole face would light up as she excitedly told us what she learned.

Montessori schools are founded on the idea that we can tap into the natural curiosity and interests of a child. By doing so, we unleash their natural desire to learn and allow them to find the best way to do so themselves.

Dr. Maria Montessori developed this idea in the early 1900s and it is still used in many schools today. She believes that when we give children the freedom to choose how they want to spend their time, they will gravitate to activities and explore ideas that fit naturally with their strengths.

Somewhere along the way in our careers and our lives, we find ourselves stepping back from making many of those choices for ourselves. Maybe we feel that we have fewer opportunities to make choices in our careers once we have committed to them. There are certainly well-worn paths that we can follow that will lead us to reasonable success, after all.

It's not that we're making fewer decisions. In fact, it is believed that we make around 35,000 decisions every day. These impact everything from what we eat and what we wear to whether we stay in a relationship. Every choice that we make takes some amount of our cognitive bandwidth. It is no wonder that we find ourselves stuck in some of the challenges that we have discussed already. We simply don't have the energy to make more choices.

Yet the choices we make will create the sustainability we are seeking. We have to become active players in creating that future for ourselves. Simply recognizing that there is always another way that we could be thinking and acting can open us up to many exciting options.

We are part of a very complex environment. Not only are all the areas in which we operate connected (by us), they are constantly changing. There is no way to know definitively how any one decision will play out. Nor can we anticipate how we may change as a result of a decision.

This is what makes navigation hard, and why there is no right answer. There are too many variables and the sand under our feet keeps shifting. We cannot rely on a static approach to navigation. Set it and forget it does not work. Autopilot can quickly lead us astray.

We have to be willing to accept the unknowns. Be curious about them as they are revealed. Follow our interests. Know who we are at the core today.

What works well for you might not work for me, and what worked for you yesterday might not have the same outcome for you tomorrow. We are constantly facing challenges that are untamed, spontaneous, organic, and complex. They are a whole different beast compared to analytical problems that we are accustomed to where a standard technique can move us steadily and reliably forward.

But do we want to be moving steadily forward at all times? Don't we want to be enjoying our journey and all the surprises that might come with it? It is in making choices for yourself that you create the journey of your dreams.

Greg McKeown, in his book Essentialism, touched on many key elements that are important to creating sustainable success. Essentialism is about choosing what is most important to you today and being fierce in creating ways to follow that. It may be necessary to explore a variety of options before you identify the best one for the current moment.

Challenges

The achievements we celebrate the most are often the ones that come the hardest. I have not met anyone yet that would say they want to have an easy life. But they do want to have a sustainable life. Sustainable does not mean boring, or unchallenging. It means that we could continue in that direction indefinitely. We have a good balance in how we are using our resources.

Given the option of a reasonable income, one with which you could meet baseline needs at $80,000 a year and be an architect, or a second option of working in a tollbooth and receiving $100,000 a year, which would you take?

My guess is you would take the first choice. Although it has a lower income, it likely offers more complexity, autonomy, and perhaps more intrinsic reward for doing creative work. Many of us have already chosen challenging careers, ones that offer us complex problems to solve and that allow us to stretch our analytical minds.

Remember Adrienne, my friend and fellow actuary, who decided to open her own consulting firm? The one thing that stuck out in our conversation was "I get to choose what challenges I will have. I might not know what they are all going to be. I am sure there will be some surprises. However, when I looked at the trajectory of the career path that I was on, I did not want to face the challenges that I saw on my path there."

She was explicitly deciding which challenges she wanted to encounter. She was not setting a course with no challenges. Some of the future battles she envisioned were ones she was willing to take on, while others were not. She was comparing them to her values, her skills, and her strengths, in order to decide which to face.

This is the case for each of us. When we look ahead at the current path that we are on, we can see some of the challenges we will need to face. We know there will be some discomfort as we do so. Yet we are often hesitant to move away from the known discomfort due to the uncertainty of what might lie elsewhere.

When we first choose our career paths, we expect to have good days and bad days. We know it won't be all rainbows, unicorns, and error-free Excel spreadsheets.

Perhaps that is why we are so willing to accept the challenges that show up along the initially chosen path. Our brain reminds us that we knew we would have challenges. When we find ourselves facing big challenges, we recall that we signed up for this. Therefore, we reason our best option is to push on through.

Because we expected challenges, we don't question whether they are the right challenges when they arrive or are looming on the horizon.

Challenges are not created equal. We may pick and choose our challenges. When we are asked to take on behaviors or engage in activities that violate our core values, we are not simply facing a challenge. We are eroding our ability to show up authentically. We are compromising our core.

These are not challenges to overcome. They are risks to our sustainability.

Other challenges encourage us to push the level of our skills or exercise areas outside of our current strengths. The best challenges we can face are what Brad Stulberg has termed "just manageable" challenges. They are above our current skill sets and abilities, but not so far that they will throw us into full-blown anxiety and stress. We can still find ways to honor our core values as we face these just manageable challenges.

When we put in the effort to think through a problem or struggle with a new idea, our brain gets to work creating new connections. The more we work at something, the more myelin is created in our brains. That myelin will strengthen and insulate the new connections. Facing the right kind of challenges is a good thing for our brains. If the challenge is too great, the stress created can start destroying the connections in our brains.

For this reason, the stresses we choose are going to either build or break down our brains. The ones that challenge our core values and who we are as a person will create more stress and ultimately cause negative growth for ourselves.

When we choose the stresses we face, we set ourselves up to be able to look at them as a challenge as opposed to strictly a source of stress. We are less likely to let them drain our enthusiasm and our energy.

Remember what your core values and principles are so you can put them first in any challenge. Temporary misalignment may be necessary as long as we keep it temporary. When we allow a challenge to put us out of alignment with our true values for the long haul, we risk losing all the benefits of growth.

Autonomy

Autonomy is, in essence, our ability to direct at least some aspects of our own lives. It is our ability to make decisions about when we choose to work, who we spend our days with, or what we spend our days doing.

Autonomy is central to creating a feeling of ownership in our lives rather than feeling like we are just along for the ride. We do not want to be puppets being directed by invisible strings, or following a predetermined course with no ability to stray.

We do not feel as engaged, interested, and excited about where we are going when we have little say in the direction. As many of those who study motivation can attest, autonomy is one of the core elements of developing and igniting intrinsic motivation.

There are many areas where autonomy can be found. Every project we work on has multiple elements defining what, who, when, how, where, and why the work is to be done. Every one of these has the potential to offer space for autonomy. There is always more than one path that will result in the desired outcome for the project.

It's not that we require control over every aspect of what we are doing. As we know, in a complex environment, there are many components that are beyond our control. When we have freedom of choice in even just a few elements of a situation, we can reap the benefits of autonomy. Who do you choose to work with? What time of day will you dedicate to getting this done? Where will you work from today?

Of course, we do not always have autonomy in every one of these areas. Many of them are limited by the external realities of a situation. We cannot always choose the team we work with or the date a project is due. Recognizing these different constraints and seeking out opportunities to choose at least one element can help us create the intrinsic motivation needed to increase our engagement in the work at hand.

Having a say in even one of these elements is a start to claiming and embracing autonomy.

Many companies are experimenting with offering more autonomy to their employees. Best Buy pioneered the ROWE (Results Only Work Environment) which allowed non-store employees flexibility in defining when and where they worked as long as they got their work done. As long as the desired results were met, employees were given autonomy to figure out how they would approach it. Later studies found that ROWE increases productivity, employee well-being, and work-life balance while reducing employee turnover.

This approach is rooted in autonomy and helps employees understand what needs to be done (the direction and outcomes that are required), and then give them the autonomy, trust, and support to accomplish the objectives in the way that works best for them.

Autonomy is a bridge to productive activity.

Our current hustle culture is all too often about busyness - staying in motion. The activities keeping us busy are often putting us on the road to unsustainability.

The idea of productive activity was coined by Erich Fromm, psychologist, and philosopher, in his book To Have or To Be.

For Fromm, to be active meant to use one's mind, talents, and personality to grow as a person. As we have already seen, this alignment with our authentic selves is a critical element in sustainability.

Productive activity is our ability to manifest our internal creativity, choice, and direction. Without the pleasure and meaning that comes from truly productive work, we lose interest in life and work. We also lose our feeling of personal responsibility for the work we do.

Through autonomy, we can reignite our interest in the work we do, and in any activity we are involved in. Using autonomy to create productive activity allows us to step away from the busyness and frenetic activity that we have gotten caught up in. We are less likely to be busy for the sake of being (or looking) busy. It allows us an opportunity to choose at least a few elements intentionally as we become more aligned and present in our actions.

Choosing our actions is a surprising way to impact our emotions and moods. When we find ourselves beginning to feel mentally and emotionally burned out in a situation, we often want to wait until we feel better so we can begin to act differently. We do not believe we have the energy to change our activities until we can shift our emotional state.

Psychological research shows that the reverse is true. Taking actions that align with your values is often a catalyst for your emotional situation to improve. By recognizing what your values are and taking actions that honor your values, you can change your mood and emotions.

Deciding

So how are we supposed to choose given the many options we start to see ahead of us? We know we want to take on challenges that will help us to grow. We can leverage autonomy in choice to improve our moods and emotional states. And we can always strive to stay aligned with our inner truths.

Dorie Clark, author of The Long Game, shares a story of a young woman who received some inspiring advice from her mother. "Whenever you have a choice of what to do, choose the more interesting path."

At some point, we begin to see the multitude of options available to us in our careers. Sometimes it comes when we walk out the door after our last day of formal education. Or maybe it waits for a pivotal point in our career. Whenever it comes, it often leaves us wondering how in the world we can possibly make a good choice.

The good news is that we aren't looking for the right choice. There is no right choice. As the number of options expands, "choose the more interesting path," is a fantastic rule of thumb to follow. Let your curiosity guide you.

Curiosity is the starting block for learning. True curiosity is intrinsically motivated. Our curiosity is driven by our interests and deep desires to learn more, see more, or understand more. It is the result of our non-conscious mind making connections and asking questions in the background.

Letting our curiosity lead us invites exploration. We allow ourselves to be led by a question, unsure about what we are going to find. We enter with fewer expectations.

Through each choice we make, we are learning more about what lights us up.

Curiosity also allows us to stay in the moment. Because we are uncertain where we are headed, the best we can do is focus on the journey.

By stepping into curiosity, we step into presence today. We are releasing our desires for the future and releasing control of the outcome. We can be both more patient with the process and present in the moment.

We, as human beings, seek meaning. We hope to belong to something bigger than ourselves. We aspire to matter. These overarching sensations are part of what defines who we are and how we see ourselves. They are longings at the heart of a life well lived.

Because there are so many choices we can make and paths we can take, believing there is one destiny for each of us to fulfill in our lives leads us directly into the right answer trap.

What if instead of a destiny, we commit to focusing on the journey? We stop looking for the path that will lead us to our purpose and our destiny. We are choosing a path each day that is creating our destiny and purpose.

Through each choice we make, we are learning more about what lights us up. We are able to make more choices that continue to light us up, and in that, we are living our purpose. Your destiny is yours to discover, not chase.

As we see more options come to light through our curiosity, our desire for autonomy, and the challenges that we foresee, there comes a point where we will have to make a decision. Decision-making is hard. Especially for the risk-averse, it can be hard to make a decision when we are not sure what we get in return.

There are two mindsets we may take on when making a decision - maximizing versus satisficing.

In decision-making, maximizers continue to put in effort to get the best possible result. They are on a mission to find the one right answer that will provide the maximum output. That answer gives them the best alignment with every single one of their criteria. Sound familiar to all you perfectionists out there?

Meanwhile, satisficers, once they identify an option that meets the base criteria, will make that their decision. They are aware that there may be better options out there, but as long as they have an option that satisfies the base criteria, they are not going to waste their energy, time, or money trying to find a marginally better option.

Satisficing is not the same thing as settling. It is founded on the recognition that there is more than one way to achieve happiness, growth, a result, or whatever it is you are seeking. A satisficer knows the value of making progress in less-than-perfect conditions.

The satisficer gets the added benefit that, by making forward progress, they are producing data. With more data, future decisions will have more information to be based on.

Satisficers recognize that choices are temporary. There is always another choice to be made.

They see the value in experimenting. Test out the different paths. Learn how they fit and how they impact sustainability.

Before you make a decision, spend time defining the characteristics that are most important to you – especially as they relate to your authentic self. List out what you want before you start looking at options. This will keep you from being influenced by the characteristics of the choices in front of you.

To create sustainability, the most important characteristics are the ones that are aligned with our values and how we desire to use our strengths and our skills.

If we wait until we have options in front of us that we are deciding on, we will be distracted by the characteristics of those options.

Knowing your values is also a very good gauge for making a decision. If we are offered a new role that would require a long commute, yet one of our core values is to spend quality time with family, perhaps that is not the right decision for us right now.

Letting your core values be a primary part of your decision process keeps you from getting distracted by shiny objects. When the most important element of your choice is alignment with your values and your sustainability, that will weigh into your decisions more than anything else.

Becoming more deliberate in the choices we make requires that we break some old habits. Especially for those of you that, like me, are people pleasers. I often offer up a resounding "Yes!" when someone starts a sentence with "Why don't we..." or "Could you...". Even before they finish the sentence I have said yes.

I was recently talking to a friend who was listing off everything he was doing – work, a side hustle, family, personal health, and the list went on and on. As we talked, it became clear that he was trying to do everything right now. He had said yes to many requests in addition to ones that he put on his own plate. He was choosing everything right now.

In the new job, he wanted to make a great impression and have quick successes associated with his name. In his side hustle, which he hopes to eventually turn into his primary hustle, he is busy writing, active on social media, creating podcasts, and planning. He has aging parents with health issues that he wants to be able to support. And I'm sure there was even more that he was not telling me.

It reminded me of a quote from David Allen, the author of Getting Things Done. "You can do anything, but not everything. "

It doesn't matter whether it is people-pleasing, overestimation of our abilities, or some other reason that brings us into the trap of saying yes. Just as we have a choice in what we say yes to, we have a choice in what we say no to. We may just need to exercise that muscle a bit.

It can be very hard to say no to something. When not saying no to things has caused us to fall out of alignment with our values or our health or the energy needs of a sustainable system, it is time to start practicing again.

Justin is a talented actuary and had become an expert in the commercial auto insurance market. Through years of participating in and then leading projects to update rates and project finances for these programs, he had become the go-to person in the consulting firm where he works.

He spent hundreds of hours each year guiding the analysis and getting up to date on changes in the markets, competition, and regulations. For many years, he loved these projects.

Justin could easily ride this success for many years. His expertise was sought out by clients and colleagues alike. And he loved the work… until he didn't. At some point, he realized he was not as engaged in this work as he used to be. He was still good at it, but he felt like he was just going through the motions.

Even so, he was hesitant to step away from it. Concerns that others might feel like he was letting them down circled in his head. How could he devalue all the time and effort he put in through the years building up this expertise? He couldn't just step aside, could he?

When I asked what he would like to spend his time on, he didn't take long to answer. He had been reading a lot recently about cyber insurance. It is a developing market with an evolving regulatory environment. In such a dynamic industry, there is never a shortage of cutting-edge ideas. He admits he would love to dive into some of these issues and think through the myriad of ways they may impact insurers and consumers alike. He would love to be a thought leader in this new frontier.

I could see him sit up straighter and become more animated when he talked about this possibility. We had found something new that energizes him. It lined up perfectly with his love of learning and sharing insights with others. He couldn't wait to be on the leading edge of market changes and helping others to make sense of upcoming complex issues.

Consistency is not a requirement.

He saw that this was a choice he could make. He could take deliberate actions to step away from his current role, which he was following by default based on his skills. He could say yes to an exciting new experiment.

He identified some capable colleagues that were eager to take bigger roles in commercial auto work. He started spending time on projects that allowed him to learn and hone new skills. He rediscovered more enjoyment and success at work. All because he made one choice. He said yes to what energized him today.

What you choose one day can be different than what you chose the day before. The key is to make it intentional. Consistency is not a requirement.

Your past achievements and knowledge do not define your future. If what interests you and piques your curiosity today is something new, make a choice to learn more and take some small but significant steps in that new direction.

When we harness the power in our choices, we are taking back some of the control in our own lives. We are breaking some of the holds that the success traps and identity traps have held us in.

We are also starting to see ways we can step out on our own. We can respond to the feelings of burnout and make choices that move us in a different direction. We can recognize when we are checking out and decide how to ignite our curiosity so we can re-engage and check back in.

You need courage to carve your path. And the tool you are carving it with is the small choice you make each day.

When we choose not to follow someone else's path, but to claim our own, we are owning the fact that our path is different. Sure, we are giving up the opportunity to blame others for potential falls along the way, but in the end, we'll find our own sustainable way through the choices we make.

Analyze This...

1. Identify one choice that you would make if you were being bold. What would you do differently if you didn't worry about the opinions of others? What would you do if you knew you would not fail?

2. Consider a challenge that you are facing. Create a mind map around that challenge. Focus on coming up with creative (not necessarily practical or obvious) paths that could address that challenge.

3. Imagine your future self. See yourself living your ideal life five years from now. What does your day look like? What are you doing? How do you feel? Identify one choice you can make today that will take you toward that vision.

Chapter 14:
EXPERIMENT

One of the final scenes of the movie La La Land shows one of the main characters, Mia, sitting in the audience at a jazz bar watching Seb, her former lover, play the piano on stage at his jazz club. They originally met and fell in love when she was a struggling actress waiting for her big break and he was a musician holding tightly to his dream of opening a jazz club. They were both chasing their dreams, pursuits that eventually took them in different directions and away from each other.

Years later, as a celebrated actress, and he as an owner of a popular jazz club, they have both created the lives they dreamed of when they were together years before.

Not only do we not know what we do not know, we cannot anticipate how we will change along our journey.

Seeing him again takes her through a vision of what life would have been like if they had made their dreams a reality while staying together. The life she envisioned with Seb might have been just as beautiful and amazing as the life she ended up living.

Every one of us has innumerable alternate realities that could have been our path. Every choice we made in our past has taken us toward one future and away from others. We are constantly choosing new adventures. Holding on to what might have been a fun diversion, but choosing new directions - big or small - today is what creates our dream life.

Ralph Waldo Emerson said, "All of life is an experiment. The more experiments you make, the better." We should never become so attached to following a path that we don't question whether we should still be on it.

As an analytical individual, I love certainty. I think in if-then statements. Much of the time this is a fine approach. I study the available data to understand the facts. With these facts, I can create a model that will get me to the answer.

That approach does not work in designing our careers and sustainable lives. Not only do we not know what we do not know, we cannot anticipate how we will change along our journey. There are too many moving parts, and our destination is not fixed.

For this reason, experimentation is a better way to look at career and life navigation. When we are focused on the journey, experimenting can open the door to opportunities we have been unaware of or afraid to consider to date.

Experimenting as you move through life means trying something different than you did the time before. It means saying yes where you may have said no before. It means following your curiosity, using your skills a little differently than you may have last time, or being a novice again.

Through experimentation, you can learn more about yourself as you observe how you react in different situations. You can get data from your emotions as you notice what you are feeling while you try something new.

Anytime someone learns that I am a coach who used to be an actuary, they often ask how I created a bridge between two very different careers. One deals very heavily with data and risk. The other with people and personal growth.

In my days as an actuary and as a senior team member, each day was full of interesting challenges and amazing colleagues. At some point, though, I started to see some signals that made me wonder whether it was time to make a change. I found myself dreaming about doing more mentoring and coaching. While there were opportunities to do more of that in my company, I wondered whether that would be enough.

I was curious about coaching. Of course, I could just take a leap of faith and make the switch. But that did not fit with my personality or my risk tolerance. As an analytical individual, I found myself wanting to experiment first. While I had an inkling of what I could do to expand my role as a mentor and guide, I wanted to get some facts before I made any switch. I was not convinced that there was a bridge from being an actuary to being a coach.

Once I knew I wanted to learn more about it, I found formal and informal opportunities to experiment. I enrolled in a course to gain an understanding of the formal coaching process and get certified as a coach. I talked with the leaders in my company to identify ways I could practice some of these skills at work. I didn't know where I was headed at that point. But I was curious enough to experiment.

Through experimentation, I was able to validate that this was something I was good at and enjoyed doing. I found myself growing my confidence and excitement about my future.

What happens when we start thinking of our life as a series of experiments?

Ironically, we gain more control. Not control of the outcome, but control of the path we are on. We have the opportunity to make more choices.

The mindset of experimentation shifts us from thinking about whether this is the right or wrong thing to do to thinking about what we are learning and how we can use that information for the next step. We are able to disconnect judgment.

Data Data Data

Experimenting creates data. And who among us is not happy about data? More data means a deeper understanding.

Much of the data we get comes from our emotions. They give us clues about what is and is not sitting well with us. We can then ask the questions to understand what it is about a situation that is bringing us joy or frustration, anger or apathy.

Even the most analytical of us are not immune to feeling emotions. Although I had gotten very good at distancing myself from my emotions. They seemed to just get in the way, slowing me down in my quest to do something. But they also tended to be there at the most pivotal times in my career and life.

As I started experimenting with career changes, the most compelling data was the emotional data. I had started the experiments because I knew there were parts of my days that didn't engage me. There were things I was spending time on that drained my mental and physical energy. I wanted to understand if there were other activities out there that could re-engage me or if this was simply the way a career was destined to evolve.

Through all of the interviews that I conducted while preparing for this book, I found that emotions and our ability to recognize them was a consistent theme and challenge.

Our bodies signal emotions differently in each of us. Interoception is the process of recognizing the internal state of the body. It is our mind making sense of the physical sensations in our bodies. Whether it is the butterflies we feel in the pit of our stomach, the headache that comes on during stress, or the jump in our heart rates, our bodies are pointing us toward the data hidden in our emotions.

Our bodies are the first place we respond emotionally to any situation. The James-Lange theory has shown that our body creates the physical response to emotions before our cognitive brain recognizes the emotion. These physical responses are being triggered by the non-conscious part of our brains.

Intuition

The idea of intuition used to be very foreign to me. As an analytical individual, I am much more comfortable looking at the facts and building from there. Intuition seemed like it lived on the opposite side of intellect.

Intuition is fast. Reasoning is slow.

Intuition is hidden. Reasoning is concrete.

Intuition refuses to show its work.

While intuition does happen in the background and it does happen quickly, it is very reliant on data. Intuition works by making connections between things we already know. For those of us that are naturally curious, love to read, research, and study, we have equipped our minds with a lot of data points to connect.

The more data you have, the better your intuition will work.

In our analytic work, we often have hunches. I can remember many times when, as I reviewed someone else's work, I could point them to a specific area for them to explore to determine why the analysis results looked funny. We can't always explain why we think a certain path is the right way, but when we trust it, more often than not we find that there was something to it. That is intuition at work.

Part of the problem with intuition for us analytical types is that it doesn't show its damn work. It is working in the background. It is making connections. And then it is giving us an answer. It is not walking us from point A to point B.

Intuition refuses to show its work. But that does not mean we should not trust it.

We do our best when our intelligence and intuition work in harmony. In fact, we solve problems more effectively when these two traits merge. It is precisely when we use the combination that we make better decisions. We strike a balance between reasoning and feeling.

Intelligent people listen to their intuition, their emotions, and their hunches. When we are experimenting, we create opportunities to explore all of these. Feelings deserve at least some of our attention. We lose insights when we invalidate them.

Listening to our emotions and our intuition can be an act of courage. Our emotions and intuition often challenge us in some way. They tend to point out a perspective different from what our intellectual mind is holding onto.

One of the ways to harness our intuition is to first recognize when it is sending us a message. Intuition signals are emotions like fear and anxiety, but also physical sensations—like feeling tense or changes in our heart rate that we can discover through interoception. They can also show up as persistent thoughts, dreams, and suspicions.

Curiosity and confusion are signals that we might need more data. They are indicators that it is time to experiment. They can come through as intuition that our body is saying there is more to be known. It cannot make a clear decision yet.

We can practice paying attention to and recognizing these signals. One of the biggest challenges of an analytical mind is knowing when to silence our reasoning mind and listen to our intuition.

Stop to gather data

Living in Colorado, I get out for hikes in the mountains often. Some of the most spectacular views can be found when hiking above the tree line, near the peaks of some of the highest mountains. Most hikes to the top of a mountain start in the trees. The trails in the trees are well marked by small placards attached to trees and well-worn paths.

Once you hit the tree line and start navigating the trail changes, the landscape changes significantly. The view is expansive. You can see far in all directions, the peaks around you, and the path in front of you. There are a lot of rocks. Sometimes the path is easy to make out through the boulders and scree. Sometimes it has faded into the rest of the surroundings.

It is at this point that you start to notice small piles of rocks alongside the path, apparently intentionally assembled (unless the marmots of Colorado are more inventive than we know). They are known as cairns, and they stand out in the landscape.

The purpose of a cairn is to keep you on the path. They are spaced far enough apart that you can see the next one when standing at the cairn you just attained. Whether the path is obvious between the cairns or not, the cairns offer clarity and smaller goals to move between as you make your way through the countryside. Once you reach one cairn, the subsequent cairn is in sight. You know what the next leg of the journey is.

Hikes in Colorado – especially those that take you to the summit of a mountain – can be very extreme. The weather changes quickly. The altitude alone can sap your energy and make what seems like an easy short hike on paper a struggle to keep moving.

Besides marking the path, cairns offer an opportunity to stop, take a breath, and look around. As you rest, replenish your energy with a drink of water and a handful of trail mix, and enjoy the view, you can also ask yourself a few key questions. Am I still on the right path? Do I see anything new from here that will make me rethink continuing with this hike?

Many times, it isn't until we get over the crest or can see around the next bend that we can make a good decision about the next part of our journey. The questions that we ask ourselves at each of the cairns are questions we can ask ourselves at any point in our careers or lives.

The cairns on a hike are a way of ensuring we are taking action and moving forward in reasonable segments as we experiment. They are also inherent opportunities to stop, review the new data we have, and reassess our goals.

What is the point of experimenting if not to gain new data? And what is the purpose of choice if not to use that new data to take ourselves in new and better directions for the moment?

We forget that our dreams and ventures can have expiration dates. Especially when there is a long path to walk before we bring them to fruition, a lot can happen in the world around us and in ourselves that makes changing the direction before we arrive a reasonable conclusion.

That does not mean that the dream or the goal of reaching that particular summit was wrong from the beginning. It simply means that our journey may not take us all the way there. We still have the benefit of everything we've experienced and learned up to that point. And we now know enough to take ourselves in a new direction that is more exciting and compelling for who we are today.

We often convince ourselves that we should stay on the path we are on simply because of what we have already put into it. Of course, the time and energy, blood, sweat, and tears we have expended are important. But it is sunk cost bias at work that makes us see those as reasons to not change course.

Sunk cost bias is our tendency to pour more resources into an activity because of what we have already put into it, rather than what we expect to get in return. The miscalculation comes from thinking that what we have put in to date has less value if we change paths, but more value if we continue on the path we're already on.

When we set time aside to pause and reconsider, we can ask ourselves what choice we would make today, from where we are now. Standing at the cairn, we can take stock of our current situation and decide where to go from here. We should celebrate how far we have come but must fight the urge to see that as the only reason to continue.

One of the more well-known approaches to experimentation was used by Google in their early days. When they first went public in 2004, they encouraged their employees to spend 20% of their time experimenting and following their interests as they worked on any idea they thought would benefit Google.

While Google's focus was on innovation, this type of approach in which you allocate a certain amount of time to experimentation offers you both a window in which to explore and permission to do just that. Especially if you are experimenting in areas that are very different from the work you do day to day, deliberately creating the space, time, and intention to experiment can ensure it happens.

You can explore your interests and see what works when the stakes are still low. Sometimes what brings you energy is completely different than what you do for your career. It can be through experimentation that you discover and grow these areas. This influx of energy can help to offset feelings of burnout in other areas.

In the sustainable system, that energy is critical. It doesn't have to come from the same arena in which you are using the energy. Because we are living a whole life, the energy created in your side hustle, in your hobby, or in time with your family can support you in your career or even carry you through the challenges of supporting aging parents.

Commitment and Goals

With any experiment we choose to undertake, it is the commitment to that decision that will make us more successful. Once we commit, we can shift our focus from the decision to the action of doing what we set out to do. Interestingly enough, commitment does more than increase our chance of success. It can also increase our happiness.

One simple study on this effect looked at an individual's satisfaction with a decision and whether or not they committed to the decision.

In the study, individuals were asked to choose a piece of art to display in their homes. One group was told that this choice was final. There would be no chance to change for another piece of artwork later. The other group was told that they could swap the artwork out at a later date.

The individuals that believed that they could not change their decision at a later date were happier with their choices. They were more satisfied in the long run with the decisions they made and had to commit to.

Once we commit, our brains start to reinforce that commitment by looking for reasons that will confirm that we made a good choice.

When we commit to actions and behaviors that are in line with our values and our natural strengths, we are also inviting our brains to support us in that decision.

Any commitment to action implies a goal has been set. And goals are wonderful motivators and ways of measuring our achievements in our progress. But there are many downsides and potential hazards when we are setting goals. We've seen a few examples already where goals can lead us astray from our values, tie us too tightly to the result and not the journey, or put us on a path towards burnout.

Goals can help narrow our focus and get clarity on activities and behaviors that will move us in the direction of the goal. However, when we make the resulting extrinsic reward the only destination that matters, we don't always find ourselves following the best route.

Attainment of certain goals may lead to ill-being. This was the case for Caroline in her drive to become the Chief Finance Officer. Achieving that big goal had led her to a role she did not enjoy, and looking at a person in the mirror she did not recognize nor particularly like.

Often, we fall into the trap of arriving at a goal and not feeling what we were hoping to feel, so we double down on the goal. We believe we did not aim high enough. We just need a bigger title or a higher income so we will feel the sense of accomplishment we are seeking.

What we may fail to recognize is that it is a time to shift. The goal we initially headed for is not the right one for us today.

The farther away a goal is set, especially if it is performance- or achievement-based, the less it should be a destination. It is more beneficial to consider it as a direction.

The defining characteristic for me is often the time between now and where that goal sits in the future. Our big dreams and our life-impacting goals are usually well in the future. These goals set our directions. But they are not yet destinations.

Each of these can be broken down into smaller actions and behaviors that move us in that direction. These can become shorter-term goals we can experiment with. These types of goals can be more task-oriented. Shorter-term goals and experiments allow us to reap the benefits of commitment while offering frequent opportunities to make adjustments as we adapt to our changing environment.

I'm not saying not to hold onto your big dreams or goals. In fact, to achieve them, you have to start somewhere. We all can have a grand vision of what we want to achieve. I encourage you to define that goal and get excited about it.

As you work towards that goal, you will make progress. You will also gain new perspectives that will help you to determine whether it is still a good direction to be heading in. Perhaps the biggest benefit of the first part of the journey is to get you far enough along that you find a big new dream to head toward.

The choices we make as experiments and learning to hold goals loosely when necessary are wonderful tools for breaking out of the right answer trap. They allow us to enjoy the process of experimentation and learn along the way.

Analyze This...

1. Start paying attention to your intuition and write down the hunches and gut feelings that you have throughout the day, whether you follow them or not. Note how the intuition showed up for you – physical sensations, emotional pulls, or other feelings. At the end of a week, review the journal and see what themes you notice. Experiment with listening to and acting on your intuition the next time it shows up.

2. Say yes. Identify an activity that you have always said "no" to or are hesitant to try and say "yes" to it. It could be something small like trying a new food, or something bigger like signing up for a class on public speaking.

3. Pick an area of your life where you want to increase your level of fulfillment or wellbeing. Identify one thing that you could do differently in this area that would take you out of your comfort zone. Commit to doing this new thing at least 20% of the time for the next month.

4. Change an element of one of your daily routines. Walk the dog on a new route. Start your daily check-in meeting with a new question for the team.

CHAPTER 15:
EXTERNALITIES

All this talk in prior chapters about choices and autonomy! It is enough to make us think that all we have to do is make a decision, take action, and make adjustments as we go. It will all work out.

And it will. I am a firm believer in the process.

Like any process, though, we have to take into account certain truths. We have to recognize the reality of our complex system.

That reality is that there are forces acting on our system that we have no control over. We have to adhere to certain rules. Just because we have decided to fly does not mean that gravity will stop acting on us.

As we recognize and acknowledge truths about ourselves, we can also see externalities and their impact on our energy, our effectiveness, and our sustainability.

Whether you prefer to see it through the lens of the serenity prayer or Stephen Covey's circle of influence concept, at the center lies control. There are and will always be elements of our lives and careers that we do not control. We can consider these as gravity, weather, and plot twists. As we will see, each of these can influence our sustainability both positively and negatively. They are not inherently bad or good.

They each influence our choices, how and when we experiment, and throw us a curveball every once in a while. They are part of what makes our focus on the journey so crucial. As weather changes and the plot twists show up, we must become adept at responding and adjusting to these shifts to maintain our sustainability (and our sanity).

Values conflicts

We often notice the negative influences of our external environment more readily than we do the positive ones. The resistance and friction we feel in certain situations can be due to a conflict with our core values. The external environment in which we operate has its own set of values. The company in which we work has an underlying culture and set of values. While a company's values can be shifted, they do not change rapidly.

A company's values are reflected in the behaviors they reward in their employees. It is reflected in expectations that are set for how we will spend our time and how we support the company. When the company's values conflict with our values, it can create a situation in which we are unable to perform effectively or efficiently. It will drain our energy. It can reduce our ability to focus and find flow. And it can make us unhappy, stressed, and burned out.

When we are clear about what our values are, we are more likely to recognize the underlying conflict. Without that clarity, we are simply left with a vague feeling that something is off.

Conflict with our values doesn't have to happen at a cultural or company level. Sometimes we encounter situations and relationships in which our values are unable to be embodied. Perhaps there is someone on the team whose values are very different from ours. When it is more temporary in nature, it looks more like the weather. We may not be able to avoid the rain for now. But we can learn how to operate sustainably in this situation.

We may notice a mismatch between our current operating procedure and what is expected of us in a new situation. We can run into gaps between our core values and those that are being reflected around us. Our actions, driven by our habits and beliefs, can be far from what is expected in a new culture. When we become aware of the gaps, we can make intentional decisions about how we want to honor our values or perhaps change some of our habits and beliefs.

What is the bottom-line impact that a lot of these externalities can have on us? When we pay attention to them, we can determine for ourselves whether they are beneficial or detrimental to sustainability and we can choose to respond appropriately. They have the potential to impact our actions, our emotions, and the options available to us.

Gravity and Weather

Recall Adrienne. In the ART of authenticity, we learned how important it was for her to work in an environment that aligned with her values. She knew she could not lead the life she wanted if she were required to conform to the culture of the company in which she was working.

In this case, the culture created an unsustainable situation for her. Adrienne recognized that the company's focus and values were significantly different from her own. The company culture was gravity. She would not be able to change it easily, and if she remained with that company, she would have to continue to work under its influence. She chose to move away from that situation.

Gravity doesn't have to be negative. It can set the stage for a more sustainable situation.

As an actuary in an international company, Amber was given a chance to take her career overseas, if only for a few years. A spot opened up in the London office and she was offered the opportunity to fill it.

As with any big decision, her analytical mind deliberated deeply before accepting the offer. The work would be similar. She was familiar and comfortable with the challenges of the job, being a leader, and managing similar projects. She knew this would be a fantastic resume builder as well.

She had been offered this opportunity based on her historical performance. She had proven herself in leading many challenging projects. It was not unusual for her to put in 60- or 70-hour work weeks as she built her career to this point.

Of course, she could do the same in another country. She had already broken the code to be successful in this company. She said yes and soon found herself on a plane.

Not long after arriving, she settled into her new role. She eagerly approached the new challenges with gusto, putting in the extra hours as needed to get the work done. She didn't realize that her manager in London was carefully watching her timecard. He sat her down one day and said "Look, Amber, you cannot be working this many hours. It's not helping your productivity. It's not allowing you to have the balance that you need with your personal life."

Was she still working for the same company? She had not anticipated a different culture within the same company.

She had developed a habit of working long hours. The company culture in the United States, if it didn't overtly encourage it, was not discouraging it. The promotions and recognition that she received reinforced her belief that this was how she was expected to work. After switching to a new culture, there was a conflict between how she was used to working and what was now expected.

It took a conscious effort to adjust to the new expectations. Eventually, she was able to reduce the time she spent at work. She found ways to become more efficient, delegate more effectively, and was able to comply with cultural expectations. She even came to love it! Never before had she had this much time for herself and her family. In this case, the result was a shift to a more sustainable approach to work. The new culture for Amber is an example of gravity moving her in a positive direction.

Every country, city, or state may have its own cultural footprint and expectations that will affect your career and your life. We may not find out what they are until we experiment with the new situation.

Gravity is non-negotiable. We cannot easily change it. We may be able to put ourselves in a new situation to escape it. Or we can find a way to coexist with it.

Weather changes more frequently. It can come and go.

"No one comes to London for the weather." The cabbie commented offhandedly, but that did not diminish the truth behind it. My husband and I had just landed in London on a dreary and wet February day. We were there for only a few days to celebrate a milestone birthday for him ahead of a work conference.

In planning the long weekend, we knew to expect clouds, chilly wind, and potentially rain at any given time. So, we set about our sightseeing bundled in jackets with an umbrella at the ready. We enjoyed the city in the opaque light from the cloudy skies. We seemed to always be walking into the wind.

When we can recognize this unwanted weather and resist the urge to control it, we can be more at peace.

We followed our own three days in London itinerary, taking in many sights we had only read about to date. We ate at Borough Market, strolled across Tower Bridge, took in a show by Piccadilly Circle, saw artifacts from every continent at the British Museum, and of course, we minded the gap.

What if we had let weather dictate the trip? We could have sat in the hotel room waiting for the sun to break through the clouds. Of course, we would have come away from the trip feeling disappointed, unfulfilled, and frustrated.

Weather is not simply a physical phenomenon. It shows up every day and impacts every situation we are in. Our daily weather might include having to deal with the slow driver in the fast lane, a client's unreasonable request to move up the deadline after they delayed their part of the project, and a leaky toilet valve that made itself known in the middle of a hectic morning.

We cannot control these elements. When we can recognize this unwanted weather and resist the urge to control it, we can be more at peace.

But weather is not always bad. Just like environmental weather, it can be splendid at times. It comes as the close-in parking space, the kind words from a colleague that make your morning, or the unexpected cancellation of the day's meetings.

Who wouldn't enjoy these moments as they show up? We can be grateful when they appear. We can even take advantage of them as they boost our energy and offer us space to be productive. They have a positive effect on our sustainability.

Whether they are good or bad, it is important to recognize that they are outside our sphere of control. We can carry an umbrella, plan to walk into the wind at times, and turn our faces to the sun when it is shining. But we cannot control the weather itself.

Plot Twists

One of Murphy's Laws states that nothing is as easy as it looks. Much of that is due to the surprises that come along as we are wandering merrily down the path we chose to experiment with.

A friend of mine loves to use the concept of a plot twist to keep her sanity during trying times when she had teenagers in the house. In reality plot twists can happen in any season of life.

There will always be completely unexpected changes in our days both at home and at work. Surprises will happen. The unexpected will happen.

It might be a fender-bender that takes your car out of commission for a week. It may be a colleague resigning at an inopportune time.

When these events happened, my friend would pause, take a breath, and yell "plot twist!"

If we try to ignore or simply do not recognize the externalities around us, their impact does not go away.

In a good novel, it is the plot twist that makes us sit up and take notice. A plot twist comes along when we've been lulled into a false sense of comfort and a sense that we know what's coming next.

The same things can happen in real life, although we don't tend to look at them as favorably as we do a plot twist in a book we are enjoying.

The plot twists of our lives are unexpected, uninvited, and often unwelcome. Again, we have a natural bias towards noticing the negative more than we might a positive plot twist. They will happen. Ignoring them or pretending they have no impact on your current path is delusional.

A plot twist turns out to be a great opportunity to sit up a little straighter and take note of what is happening around us. We can make adjustments for what we notice at that time. They often remind us to pause and look around.

In the context of gravity and weather, the plot twist is like the lightning strike or the tornado that hits somewhere out of the blue. Similar to gravity and weather in our system, our sustainability is best served by acknowledging the impact it has on us and responding appropriately.

If we try to ignore or simply do not recognize the externalities around us, their impact does not go away. Whether we see them clearly or not, we will feel both the positive and negative effects on our sustainability.

We don't get to choose the gravity, weather, or plot twists in our system. But when we are aware of them and respond to them deliberately, we can make better choices for our sustainability.

Analyze This...

1. Consider your core values identified in other exercises. Identify the values in this list that are non-negotiable. Also indicate which you might be willing to compromise on in the right situation, at least temporarily. Look at your current work and life situations. Identify any places where your "must not violate" values are at risk of being violated. Identify one action you might take to honor that value.

2. Write a letter to yourself from the perspective of a trusted friend or colleague, acknowledging the things that you cannot control but expressing admiration for the way you navigated them.

3. List the various challenges of a current situation. For each element, indicate whether it is something that you can control, something that you can influence, or something that is outside your influence. Focus your actions on the items in the first two categories.

SECTION 6:
HELP YOUR BRAIN HELP YOU

There are two types of people in this world: 1) Those who can extrapolate from incomplete data sets.

In the end, we will never have complete data with which to create our sustainable lives. But we do have the tools we need to help our brains along the way.

Even though our brains share some of the blame for getting us into this mess, they are also the perfect partner to help get us out. They are key to bringing sustainability into our lives. We just need to nudge them a little bit. Like a child that is drawing on the wall rather than on paper, there are ways to constructively redirect our brains.

We know how we can show up more authentically and have more confidence in our choices and experiments we will undertake along the journey.

Now we get to encourage our brain to become our ally again. We can direct our analytical mind's superpower of identifying patterns in the newly available data, identifying the best ways to motivate ourselves more effectively in different situations, and set up our environments to support our brain's and body's health and wellbeing.

CHAPTER 16:
PATTERNS

One of the superpowers we, as individuals with analytical minds, have is that we are built to recognize and ferret out patterns. In everything. Even when we don't think we're paying attention, our subconscious is busy making note of commonalities and differences, seeing trends, and ordering information. We thrive on making sense of the chaos.

When we get data, one of the best things we can do is unleash that skill. Our brains will simplify the complex. They can see trends and raise questions about patterns that appear.

And we know that we can do it because it is often the cornerstone of our past achievements in our careers.

Now we get to direct that natural ability more intentionally toward our careers and lives. Put on your analyst hat. Take a look at the data you have. What is it telling you?

An Analytical Mind's Superpower

When I was feeling the first pangs of uncertainty - and fear - about whether I was in the right place in my career, or whether it was time to pivot, I found myself falling back on analytics. I had so many questions about what I enjoyed doing and where I got my energy. The best thing to do was to capture some data that would help me to answer those questions.

I spent two weeks tracking my time. Yes, it was one more thing to add to my list of to-dos each day. But knowing that this was part of my path to a more sustainable life, I committed to the two-week exercise. I wasn't sure what I would find. But I knew that with actual data, I had a much better chance of finding the insights that could get me unstuck.

In 15-minute increments, I would make a note of what I was doing during the day - at work, at home, and everywhere in between. I noted when I had a conversation with a client regarding questions we had about their data. When I was building a spreadsheet to review a colleague's analysis. When I was having lunch with a peer. When I was at the grocery store or relaxing with a book at home. For each element, I would score my engagement levels. Was I highly engaged in the activity, or just going through the motions? I paid attention to whether I came away with more or less energy than I went in with, or if it was energy neutral.

At the end of two weeks, I had a lot of data. Even as I was in the process of creating the data, I could see patterns starting to form. I was noticing that being a part of conversations that grew others was very engaging and energizing for me. I walked away from those, whether they were five minutes or two hours, with more energy than I started with, both at work and at home.

I could see the times when I was just going through the motions, falling back on skills I had gained throughout my career, but ones that did not light me up as much anymore. These times looked successful on the surface because I was being productive and achieving project goals. Based on my engagement levels and the drain they created for my energy, though, they were contributing to some of the unsustainability I was feeling. While I still enjoyed working with my team to resolve technical challenges, I didn't get much out of being too far in the weeds.

As you experiment with your path, you will be constantly gathering new data. As we noted earlier, when we view our decisions as experiments, we are naturally in the mindset of collecting data.

We can also look back at other information we have gathered. For example, multiple companies I worked for encouraged employees to take the Clifton Strengths assessment, the Myers Briggs personality indicator, or the Values in Action (VIA) survey. Each of these (and many others) offer snapshots of your strengths, personality traits, and values. They can be great additions to the data that you are collecting.

Every interaction we have, compliment we are paid, or request to help someone else can bring with it data for us to better understand ourselves and the way that others see us. They exemplify the skills, strengths, and talents that come naturally.

By reflecting on highlights and notable memories from my career, I found one very telling piece of data that confirmed some of the patterns I was uncovering today.

When I had just started out in my career as an actuarial analyst for a large insurance company, I was invited to be a part of a leadership training event. It was an opportunity to step out of our analytical roles and begin to develop some of the soft skills needed to become an effective leader. The facilitators led us through impactful exercises and discussions.

It was an enlightening training and I, for one, was getting a lot out of it. Everyone in the room seemed to be engaged and actively participating (not a small task when most everyone is an introvert).

At some point in the day, my friend and fellow actuary leaned over to me and whispered, "I have a feeling you're supposed to be up at the front of the room."

It was not what I was expecting to hear. And it was not something that I, who just embarked on a brand-new career to be an actuary, necessarily wanted to hear. I filed it away as just an odd little insight that meant nothing.

Decades later, that little insight was one of the data points that cemented my choice to experiment in a new direction. We never know where the data points will come from.

Pitfalls

As with any analysis, it's important to keep in mind that there may be biases influencing our results and our data.

The peak-end bias is our tendency to remember and judge experiences based on how we felt during the peaks (the highs and the lows of the experience) and in the final moments of the experience.

Especially when we are looking back at a situation, rather than tracking data in 15-minute increments, this bias can come into play. It is probably the reason I recalled my friend's oddball comment to me during that training years ago.

Think about a close football game. It is coming down to the last 30 seconds of the game and your favorite team is only two points down. They have the ball and have been unable to get a touchdown. Here they sit at third down and five, with a long but doable field goal.

I always feel for the kicker at this point. The game comes down to how well he performs. He might have made every single extra point and multiple other field goals already. None of that will matter if he does not make this last field goal. Not a soul will be talking about anything but the final attempt. How people will feel about the whole game will be shaped by this one kick.

The same happens even in mundane activities such as driving to work. We have smooth sailing through green lights for the first half. Our favorite station is keeping us company as we drum our fingers along with the beat on the steering wheel. All of a sudden, another driver bolts into the lane ahead of us, giving us just inches to avoid their bumper. As we hit our brakes, glancing in the rear-view mirror to make sure we aren't going to get hit ourselves, the driver shifts over to the turn lane and obviously disappears from view. The rest of the drive, although uneventful, is spent flexing our fingers to release the tension we had created.

Our brain tends to connect with that negative event, even though it was only one minute out of our twenty-minute drive. Our memory of the drive is tarnished by this one low event. It is the story we share with our spouse when we get home, not bothering to mention all the green lights we enjoyed.

Peak-end bias has corrupted our memories. Our data is not as clean as we might hope.

I can see one benefit to peak-end bias. Whether highs or lows, our emotions are most engaged during the peaks. And our emotions often point to our values and our personality. Scrutinizing the peaks and valleys of our experiences may help us to identify our core values, natural strengths, and certain elements of our personality.

Hidden Insights

The patterns we should be seeking out are those that will offer us insight into our next experiment. We are looking for patterns that we can either disrupt or exploit so we can break out of the traps that are holding us in place today and create more sustainable paths.

Creating a sustainable life is not a distant experiment, but one in which we are active, integral, and important characters.

These traps, especially our connection to past successes and holding on to surface-level identities, were created and reinforced by patterns. Our brains hold on to the repeated achievements that make up the paradigm of success we have become so closely connected with.

As we look into the data more deeply, we will identify new patterns. We can see the building blocks that led up to our past successes, we might see the actions, interests, talents, and mindsets that carried us to success. These are the transferable elements. Once we see them more clearly, we can use them as building blocks to create the new future we desire today.

As with any challenging puzzle, the patterns may not reveal themselves immediately. We should be prepared to give ourselves space and time for the patterns to emerge. Especially since the patterns that matter most are not on the surface. Our subconscious brains will need time to tease out the building blocks that created our past. No spreadsheet or statistical analysis will offer the same insights.

As David Goss, PhD, an American mathematician noted, "The subconscious is a crazily powerful thing. It's almost like the sole reason you do the work is to set the stage for what happens when you step away." The work we do is to identify the raw data. Then we get to step away and wait for the patterns to emerge.

Although to some degree we are analyzing data like a scientist, we are also not impartial observers in the process. Creating a sustainable life is not a distant experiment, but one in which we are active, integral, and important characters. We have the ability and the obligation to influence the results.

As we look back at the data, we may see some building blocks that created negative outcomes or that played a direct role in setting us on an unsustainable path. As we notice these showing up today, we are better equipped to interrupt the pattern.

Some of us are serial job hoppers, moving from job to job and company to company in search of the greener grass that we believe is just one decision away from discovery. There are many reasons we may be jumping from job to job. One of us may be avoiding difficult conversations while another may be following our competitive nature as we always want to one-up our colleagues. Perhaps our desire to provide a financially secure future has us following higher-paying positions even after we have attained a comfortable lifestyle.

When we see these patterns, we can be more intentional about breaking the cycle and redirecting the power of our values and interests into a more sustainable future.

Analyze This...

1. Write down in detail how you spent your time at home and at work each day for a week. Review the list and highlight the items that directly relate to your current priorities. Search for patterns in the comparisons.

2. Look for patterns in your actions in the last 3 months. Based on what you are noticing, what might a good area be to experiment in next?

3. Work your pattern recognition muscle by playing games that require you to recognize patterns, such as Sudoku or jigsaw puzzles.

CHAPTER 17:
MOTIVATION

"People often say that motivation doesn't last. Well, neither does bathing - that's why we recommend it daily"- Zig Ziglar

Something motivated you to do every single thing you did yesterday, whether or not you were consciously aware of what the specific motivation was. In fact, it is often hard to name exactly what is motivating us because it is not one thing. Our actions are the culmination of multiple influences and motivations pushing and pulling in the background.

Yesterday's snack of apple slices was motivated in part by a physical feeling of hunger and a desire not to wither away and die. It was also driven by the procrastination coming from my underlying frustration with a project and lack of clarity on my next steps. The choice to have an apple rather than a bowl of Nutella was influenced by my desire to be healthy. One action, many motivations.

With all this going on in the background, how can we possibly tease out what is motivating us so that we can use it to create the future we desire?

Our motivations are the drivers behind our actions. They are part of the system that makes up our lives and our careers. There is no one motivation that will be the key to your future. When we understand the different types of motivations and how they can influence our actions and our mindset, we can be smarter about using them to move us toward sustainability.

As we discover the deeper patterns emerging through our experiments and our experiences, we may start to see how different motivations affect our behaviors.

The prevailing belief used to be that there were two drivers of behavior - biological needs and responses to external reinforcements or punishments.

In the 1940s, primate psychologist Harry Harlow and colleagues set out to discover how rewards and punishments impacted learning in rhesus monkeys. They planned out an experiment to guide the monkeys through the process of learning how to solve a simple three-step physical puzzle.

As part of the preparation for the experiment, they placed the puzzles into the cages with the monkeys. They intended to give the monkeys a few weeks to adjust to having a strange object near them so that any potential fear would not taint the results of their experiment.

They ended up stumbling on what would become a cornerstone in the study of motivation.

With the puzzles now in the cage, the monkeys started exploring them. There was no biological need for them to do so. No apparent benefit to them. No treats were given. No punishment was inflicted. They were simply allowed to coexist with the puzzle, and they took it upon themselves to interact with it and explore it.

By the time the intended experiment rolled around, many had already solved the puzzles.

A new driver was added to the scientific understanding of motivation: intrinsic motivation.

More is being learned all the time about motivation and what drives our behaviors. I believe our best approach as we look to use motivations as part of our sustainable journey is to understand the basics about each of them, learn how we can recognize them in our own lives, and experiment intentionally with our motivations. After all, our motivations are as unique as we are, and they change with us as we evolve through our lives.

One type of motivation is not inherently better than another although they play distinct roles in creating a sustainable life. As we understand motivation more deeply, we can be better equipped to motivate ourselves in different ways for each unique situation.

Every behavior and action has some sort of motivation behind it, and often a combination of many motivators. We will explore three motivations: extrinsic, intrinsic, and identity-based motivation.

Extrinsic Motivation

Extrinsic motivation drives by way of an external reward (or deterrent). These are the paychecks, the praise, the criticism, the grades, or anything that comes your way from somewhere outside of yourself.

With extrinsic motivation, we behave a certain way because of the payoff or pain we anticipate. The act itself does not provide us with any reward.

Extrinsic motivations have different utilities in different situations. There is often a baseline level of rewards, especially monetary ones, below which we will feel more motivated to make a change. Recall our earlier example of choosing between a role as an architect for a salary of $80,000 versus a toll booth operator with a salary of $100,000. For many people, the baseline of $80,000 may be enough to meet their needs for housing, food, and other necessities so the extrinsic motivation may not be too strong. The decision would likely be very different if choosing between $40,000 and $60,000 salaries for the same professions.

I leaned a lot on extrinsic motivation when pushing myself to complete the series of professional exams on my way to becoming a fully certified actuary. At the beginning of my actuarial career, there were well-defined changes in my title and my salary that would come with every exam that I passed. That, alone, was enough to keep me focused on studying many Saturday evenings when part of me would have preferred relaxing at a movie or even doing the dishes.

Extrinsic motivation encourages us to "keep our eyes on the prize." This type of motivation can very well work on short-term goals and algorithmic type of tasks with a fairly clear process and resulting outcome. The rewards can offer a motivational boost and a reason to continue with the activity when it is boring, routine, or repetitive. The main goal in these cases is the completion of the activity.

There are many limitations to what we can accomplish with extrinsic rewards, though. Extrinsic motivation may create a situation where we let the ends justify the means. When the completion of a goal triggers the external reward, the path we choose to take becomes less relevant. We may take shortcuts or even dishonor our principles and values if the external rewards are great enough. This, though, can lead to mental and emotional stress which can start us on the path to burnout.

My theory is that we, as analytical individuals, can become preoccupied with measuring our progress and analyzing the chance that we're going to get that reward. The larger the reward, the higher desire to get it. And the less we pay attention to the actual task at hand.

Additionally, studies show we will generally only work to the point that the extrinsic reward is offered. If a student receives a prize for reading ten books, they often do not bother to pick up an eleventh one once the prize is delivered. We are operating under a very clear if-then paradigm. Certain actions or results beget certain rewards.

In 1969, Edward Deci, a Carnegie Mellon University psychology graduate student found that while external rewards - such as money - can provide a short-term boost for an activity, their effect will wear off over time. The same student, when offered the same prize for reading another ten books, is less likely to participate a second time.

Later studies by Mark Lepper and David Greene show that extrinsic rewards can even reduce the impact of intrinsic motivation. In their work, they observed how frequently preschool students chose to draw pictures when materials were available to them during their free time. During the experiment, some of the children were offered specific rewards for each drawing they completed, others received unexpected rewards, and a third group did not receive any rewards.

Once the reward was removed again, they watched to see whether the children still chose to draw on their own. An interesting outcome was observed. The students that were offered explicit rewards for their drawings were less likely to draw at later playtimes. Those that either received unexpected awards or received no award at all were just as likely to continue drawing just for the fun of it.

The external rewards had reduced the apparent intrinsic desire to draw.

As we perform tasks that are intrinsically motivating, we often find that we are creating energy that keeps us going.

Even though there are limitations to extrinsic motivation, in the right situations, we can use it as an effective tool to engage our focus and create drive when intrinsic motivation is not present or when we have a short-term, algorithmic task ahead of us.

Intrinsic Motivation

The American Psychological Association defines intrinsic motivation as "an incentive to engage in a specific activity that derives from pleasure in the activity itself (e.g., a genuine interest in a subject studied) rather than because of any external benefits that might be obtained (e.g., money, course credits)." That is, we do it just because.

Like the rhesus monkeys exploring the puzzles in Dr. Harlow's experiments, there is no apparent benefit from the outside. There is no telling with the monkeys whether it was curiosity, a feeling of fun, or something else that drove them to investigate the puzzles. We only know that it came from within.

Within ourselves, we might have more insight into what we are feeling. We often enjoy the opportunity to explore, learn, and actualize our potential. Our drive comes from connecting to our interests and core values and using strengths, among other things. The rewards we receive come through the sense of meaning or progress we experience. We may be rewarded with a higher level of competence in a subject we love, or a new skill. Or it might just be fun.

As we perform tasks that are intrinsically motivating, we often find that we are creating energy that keeps us going. We create a sustainable cycle.

Did you ever have a project in school that you just didn't care about? One that you had to talk yourself into completing or push yourself with external rewards just to get through.

Now compare that to a project you were interested in. My guess is you jumped in without much effort. You found yourself going down rabbit holes of research. The challenge might have been in keeping yourself constrained to the limits of the assignment.

We tend to be more creative when we are intrinsically motivated. We eagerly explore new angles and ask more creative questions about the challenge we are facing.

The difference between the two comes from within. The inherent interest in a project or a topic creates the intrinsic motivation to dig in further. You find yourself energized when working on the project. The work becomes satisfying and rewarding as you learn more about the topic, expand your current skillset, and get to decide how you approach each phase of the work. Your ability to focus decreases distractions and increases both creativity and productivity. As a sustainable machine, we can feel the momentum increasing.

When we are involved in tasks that are intrinsically motivating, we have the potential of finding ourselves in flow.

Flow is a psychological term describing a state in which you are fully engrossed in what you are doing. The idea of flow was coined by psychologist Mihaly Csikszentmihalyi in the 1980s. It is the feeling of losing yourself in a challenging task. You know the task - the one that you look up from and are surprised that two hours have passed in what feels like minutes.

Flow happens when we are challenged above our current skill set, but not so much that it induces anxiety. We have been able to eliminate distractions. Flow allows us to not only benefit from the intrinsic motivation that is getting us there and fueling the process, but we may be much more productive in that state. By tying into intrinsic motivation, we can harness this amazing power.

Our open-source world today is a prime example of this. Working on an open-source project gives us many opportunities to let our intrinsic motivation decide what we want to work on. People jump into what they are curious about and what they see as a challenge, whether it is an open-source cookbook, software coding challenge, or creating stock photography.

Research by Professor Karim Lakhani at MIT and Boston Consulting Group consultant Bob Wolf found that individuals who contributed to open-source projects reported that they frequently found themselves in flow. I envision the blue light of a computer screen glowing on the contributor's face in a dark room as they work long into the night for the simple joy of creating. There is no obvious extrinsic motivation for open-source. It is powered by curiosity, challenge, and enjoyment.

Daniel Pink offers three main elements that are present in intrinsic motivation. These are autonomy, mastery, and purpose.

Autonomy is our ability to choose for ourselves what we want to be doing. We get to have some say in the matter. We have a choice.

We all value having some control over our time, energy, and what we do each day. Even if we cannot choose every element, having some autonomy to decide who we work with, when we are putting in our time, where we work, and the like may be enough to ignite intrinsic motivation.

With the control we are afforded through autonomy, we can connect more easily with the elements of the project that pique our interest, align with our values, fit our strengths, or otherwise reflect our authenticity. We get this through even small levels of independence in the project.

Mastery is our ability to challenge ourselves, expand our performance, and learn. We don't want an easy road. We get to mastery through the challenges we choose. Csikszentmihalyi noticed this in his studies of flow. It is the challenge that puts us into flow. We become inspired through the satisfaction of pushing ourselves a little more.

Purpose is the desire to have an impact and be a part of something bigger than ourselves. It ties back to our authenticity and being true to our core values, which frequently include an element of impact or purpose in them. The purpose connects us to the why behind our actions.

In 2009, in response to recent economic challenges created in part by decisions made by financiers and corporate dealmakers, a group of Harvard MBA students created a new "MBA Oath." Similar to the medical profession's Hippocratic oath, it was a pledge to follow certain conduct guidelines. It starts with a direct tie to service and purpose, "As a manager, my purpose is to serve the greater good by bringing people and resources together to create value that no single individual can create alone." Even in the famously cutthroat world of business and finances, there is room for and a need for purpose.

Identity-based Motivation

A third type of motivation, and one that is related to intrinsic motivation is identity-based motivation.

This is a social psychological theory of human motivation and goal pursuit. It offers the idea that people's identities can motivate them to behave a certain way. The theory assumes that we will act and think in ways that are congruent with the identity that we hold in our minds.

We believe we know who we are. And who we are matters for what we do. Lucky for us, our self-concept does not need empirical support. That is, we can claim the identity of a healthy person before we start acting like one. Our brain will not automatically reject the identity.

An individual's self-concept will motivate them to take or not take action toward their goals. Depending on which identities we place at the forefront, we will assess whether an action is congruent with that identity. If we see the situation as incongruent with our identity, we are likely to conclude that the behavior is "not for people like me," so we avoid it. When it is congruent, we will take action. For example, when your identity as a healthy individual is front and center, it is easier to get up at 5 AM to go to the gym. If the identity you put forward for yourself is that of a hard worker in your career, the motivation for the gym in the early morning will be harder to find.

The identities we define can be personal or social. They can be tied to relationships or roles or even in association with specific groups. We hold onto multiple identities at one time. Our minds begin to focus on whatever identities we hold as stable.

Identity-based motivation is why many theories of positive self-talk and picturing yourself as the individual you want to be can be so powerful. We can fool our brains into holding that identity well before all of our actions align with it.

Identity-based motivation can also help explain why we fall into the identity trap so easily. When we tie our identity to a title or a role, we are encouraging our brain to seek out only actions and activities that are congruent with that specific and narrow definition of who we see ourselves as. With an identity that comes from our achievements as opposed to our core values, we can easily find ourselves running the wrong race.

Of course, there are many more theories on motivation. These three are some of the more common and easy to recognize. We are not pursuing a psychology Ph.D., but rather a way to frame how we look at and engage motivation.

When you enjoy what you are doing, motivation is easy to find. The reward comes in the doing, not in the result of a paycheck or a promotion. Liking what you do makes the work itself feel easier. Gallup researchers found that highly engaged employees work more hours than their counterparts, likely because they are finding inspiration and enjoyment in the work itself.

When you like what you do, you do more of it, which creates greater competency and higher rewards (both intrinsic and extrinsic). It's a virtuous cycle of personal growth and professional development; the journey becomes rewarding. The work may be hard, but the hard work feels worth it.

As we understand what motivates us most effectively, we can use that information to set ourselves up for sustainable success. We can create opportunities to encourage states of flow, consciously choose identities that will make it easier to live as we would like to, and use extrinsic motivations wisely.

Intrinsic motivation certainly rises to the top as one of the more powerful tools. There are ways we can tap into intrinsic motivation more easily. We have already talked about a few of these as they are some of the elements Dan Pink notes.

By increasing our level of autonomy available in an activity, we can find ways that suit our desires and needs best. We do not have to have full autonomy. We can get some of the benefits just by having a say in a few elements of a task.

When we can engage in behaviors and activities that challenge us beyond our current skill set, we can tap into intrinsic motivation through mastery. We are not aiming for ultimate mastery, but rather moving to the next just manageable level. This encourages constant growth as well.

When we can clearly see congruency between our behaviors and the core values that we hold, intrinsic motivation is engaged. To do this, though, we have to be clear on what our core values are and how we define them today. There are many simple and effective exercises available to get clarity on our core values.

By simply writing down our core values and keeping them where we can regularly revisit them and be reminded of them, we can shift our focus from other metrics. Writing it down signals our brain that this is important and should be paid attention to.

We have seen that our intrinsic motivation can be affected by the presence of external rewards. To minimize this impact, if avoiding the use of external rewards is not feasible, at a minimum ensure that the external reward happens close to the activity.

Sometimes our intrinsic motivation cannot be engaged because it is being undermined by unmet needs elsewhere. When we are sleep-deprived, hungry (or hangry), or distracted by multiple competing goals, we cannot fully focus on what we want to do, no matter how strong the internal drive is.

To reinforce the rewards we want to be using as drivers, we can intentionally encourage our brains to notice those. By bringing our intrinsic motivation to the forefront, we can train our brain to see the value in creating joy and behaving congruently with our core values or concordant with our identities. All of this can be done through the practice of celebration and gratitude. When we consciously express our gratitude for choosing to go to the gym because we are healthy, we are letting our brains know what to pay attention to. We are training it to move towards the behaviors we decide are important.

Finally, recognize that time discounting is a bias that impacts our motivation. This phenomenon causes us to take a known reward now rather than wait for a bigger benefit in the future. In a way, it is the adult version of the famed "marshmallow test" that indicates children's willpower and future success in life.

With this bias, we do what feels good in the moment today and do not work the muscle that builds the habits that will get us better results in the future. We are underestimating the long-term value of starting sooner rather than later.

When we can clearly identify with our future selves, we can offset some of the bias at work here. In fact, if we do not find ways to motivate ourselves to create some good behaviors today, it is our future self that will be feeling the weight of those choices in the coming years.

Analyze This...

1. Consider a current goal that you are excited about pursuing. Ask yourself why you want to do it. Whatever your answer, ask yourself "why" again and then again. What does this reveal about your deepest motivators? Think of ways that you can use a similar motivator (your reason behind your deepest "why") for an activity that you are struggling to get excited about.

2. Imagine yourself as your ideal self. List out what motivates that version of you. What kind of values and strengths does that identity lean on? Consider your current self, identify the areas where your motivations in place today are different or the same as those your ideal self would respond to.

3. Keep a gratitude journal. Every day, write down a few things that you are grateful for and why. Periodically, look back at the things that you have been grateful for to discern any patterns in how those make you feel, what joy or energy they bring, and other clues to your intrinsic motivators.

CHAPTER 18:
SUPPORT YOUR BRAIN

"Follow your heart but take your brain with you." - Alfred Adler

I prefer to think of this quote a little differently. I believe our brains can lead us on the path where our hearts long to go. The trick is equipping our brains for the task, which we can do in part by creating a healthy and supportive environment for them.

I'm always looking for a good hack. I love to discover and employ shortcuts to make everyday challenges a little easier. With hacks, it is not about finding one overarching solution that will make all the challenges go away, rather, it is about implementing a variety of small changes that nudge us onto and along a better path.

As I was writing this book, I discovered that reading for 10 minutes was a powerful way to prime my brain for writing. When I took the time to do it, I noticed that the words tended to flow a little more freely. I had more ideas and could be more creative in connecting them.

It got me wondering whether there were ways we could prime our brains to help them create the sustainable life we desire. As we have seen already, our brains are critical partners in living authentically, choosing paths to experiment with, and identifying patterns. It can do all of this more effectively and efficiently if we help it along.

There are hundreds of small ways we can set ourselves up for success. That is what hacking the brain is about. Many ways that improve the health of our bodies have a similarly beneficial impact on the brain. There are also ways we can design our environments that encourage our brains to work creatively and efficiently. We are asking a lot of our brains, and we will need to give them space to do the heavy lifting.

A Healthy Brain

The first thing we can do to keep the system well and functioning sustainably is to focus on basic care. Our physical health and our brain health are the same. It makes sense, of course, I have yet to meet a human whose brain is completely disconnected from their body (although at times on the tennis court, I might be a prime example).

There are plenty of studies that show a distinct benefit to our brains from the same activities that improve our physical health.

Physical movement and exercise can be significantly transformative for your brain and its ability to function well. Physical activity increases creative thinking and problem-solving, improves mood and emotional control, enhances focus and energy, and promotes quality sleep. All of these are activities of a healthy brain.

Our brains rely on many neurotransmitters including serotonin, norepinephrine, and dopamine to think, regulate emotions, remember, and reason. Each of these chemicals regulates different elements. For example, serotonin assists with mood, norepinephrine increases perception, and dopamine regulates attention and satisfaction. While we won't go into brain chemicals in detail (there are plenty of books you can read that will take you as deep as you want), what is key is that they need to be in balance, or our cognitive and emotional capacities will suffer.

Exercise can have an immediate effect on balancing the neurochemicals that our brains depend on. When we move our bodies, we release these neurochemicals. Studies have shown that even a 10-minute walk can improve mood and heighten creativity.

The type of physical activity does not matter. It is your choice. Love tennis? Call up your favorite partner. Enjoy a bike ride? Grab your helmet and start pedaling. Just want some one-on-one time with your dog? Head to the park with them. This one also keeps your furry friend happy.

Quality sleep is necessary for our brains as well. Our brains stay very active while we sleep. During sleep, our brains get busy removing toxins that can affect memory, learning, and emotional regulation. It also works to modulate our immune system and process our memories.

Many of our presumed intuitive decisions come through insights gained during sleep. We are able to solve many challenging problems that eluded us during our conscious waking time. Just think about the last time you went to sleep after struggling to have a breakthrough on a challenging problem only to wake up with clear insights on what the next steps are.

Sleep is a simple way to improve the functioning of our brains. Many studies observe the effect of blue light that we are exposed to from the screens of our computers and smartphones, as well as other stimulants we subject our brains to before nodding off. All of these can reduce the quality of sleep and make it harder for our brains to do what they need to do during sleeping hours. Combine the reduction in quality sleep with the reduction in the number of hours of sleep that we have seen over the past 70 to 80 years, and we find ourselves depriving our brains of one thing that will make us more productive during the day.

Supportive Environments

The environment around us is often something we take as a given or otherwise overlook. We are too busy focusing on what we are doing to give much thought to where we do it. We do not think about the impact the space around us has on our brains. At best, we treat them as independent, and we strive to be in an environment that makes us physically comfortable. At worst, we treat the environment as a nice to have and put up with environments that are less than ideal for us.

There are concrete benefits for our brains that we tap into simply by tweaking our environments. For anyone who, like me, is solar-powered, we can see very easily which environments will have a negative impact. If you ask me to work in a room with no natural light, it will quickly turn into a Dr. Jekyll and Mr. Hyde situation. Natural light helps me regulate my mood.

Our brains know our bodies are meant to have a connection to the living world beyond us.

Whether we are designing the space we work in or simply taking advantage of environments and opportunities around us to put ourselves into nature, where we spend our time has a significant impact on our brains' ability to function.

Let's start with nature. This is the first environment our ancestors knew. It still has a very profound impact on our monkey brain's ability to work effectively. In the book The Extended Mind, Annie Murphy Paul shares many examples of studies that explore the impact that nature has on our ability to think well.

Researchers have found that nature is a reliable and effective drug for our brains and our bodies. Within less than one minute of being exposed to nature, our heart rates slow and our blood pressure drops. Our brain activity becomes more relaxed. We gaze longer and blink less often when viewing nature than when we are observing elements in an urban setting. Simply being in nature is less cognitively taxing than being in manmade settings.

It is believed that our brains subconsciously respond to the fractal characteristics of natural scenes. These patterns impact our brains at a deep level. They are found in everything from plant structures to clouds, sand dunes, ocean waves, and tree canopies.

Our brains know our bodies are meant to have a connection to the living world beyond us.

While all of this can be found by taking ourselves into nature, if you are not in a location where you can find trees and wandering paths waiting for you just outside your front door, do not despair. Bringing nature indoors through the presence of plants can increase and improve your attention and memory as well as your productivity levels.

In Japan, scientists have taken hundreds of individuals on forest walks through lush green spaces. Before and after the walks, researchers measured multiple bio indicators related to stress. These forest walks demonstrated greater positive impacts than walks of the same duration in an urban setting. They reduce stress levels and diminish the sympathetic nerve activity in the brain.

This may have influenced University of Chicago psychologist Marc Berman and doctoral student Kathryn Schertz as they developed an app called ReTUNE in 2017 as part of a university app development challenge. Berman's research had shown that maximizing exposure to natural elements while walking in an urban setting can improve attention, memory, and mood. They created a GPS application that would show walkers the optimal route from one point to another so they could arrive more clear-headed and relaxed.

ReTUNE is based on the premise that it is not the speed of the journey but what you encounter along the way that will improve mental well-being.

Nature also provides an opportunity to experience awe. Awe is the feeling of vastness and the sense of being in the presence of something that straddles the boundary of pleasure and fear. Awe can come from moments of seeing incredible vistas in nature or even witnessing a touching act of kindness.

Dacher Keltner's research shows that awe is also important for our well-being. Besides the physical responses of calming our nervous system, it can release oxytocin, which is the chemical that promotes trust and bonding. It can reduce the stress that prohibits us from performing at our peak.

It can reduce the feeling of self-preoccupation. We see ourselves as a smaller part of the bigger picture. We are able to take some of the weight off of our shortcomings. We gain perspective.

Experiencing awe can reorient our values. Even though our core values are relatively stable, we can sometimes find ourselves in situations that have caused us to be more egocentric or materialistic than we would like to be. At these times, we may realize that we have become disconnected from our core values, especially the ones that define the impact on the greater world we hope to have. By placing ourselves in situations that induce awe, we can move those core values closer to the surface and our conscious awareness.

With all this science showing that our brains respond differently when exposed to nature, it's hard not to deliberately invite in more of the outdoors. It is up to you if you want to move to a hut in the woods, place a plant on your desk, or do something in between. We can choose to use the benefits that are already hardwired within us.

As much as I would love to have a fully outdoor office in which I could be one with nature at all times, it isn't realistic (and not only because my computer is not waterproof). We work in built spaces. We sit at desks with bookshelves around us and certificates framed on the walls. In these days of virtual work, we may even be sharing space with a sleeping or eating area.

In the spaces we curate for ourselves, we can bring in some nature. But there are other things we can do to nudge our brains.

The items we choose to place around us are important. Look around your workspace the next time you are there. What do you see? I see a tree behind me and a few plants, complete with a corny plant stake saying, "Wet my plants." Of course, there are bookshelves full of books. My wall holds a calendar that allows me to stay organized at a glance. There are small gifts from my girls and a few fidgety gadgets to keep my hands busy during calls.

What you have in your space might reflect your creativity, achievements, or quirky sense of humor. They may also serve a specific purpose.

We place objects intentionally so that others can see them and learn something about us, or we may keep some objects visible only to ourselves. A study in the Academy of Management Journal examined the workspaces of people holding a variety of jobs. About a third of the workspace objects were positioned such that only the individual could see them. Most of these objects had a stated purpose of reminding them of their goals and values. They were intentional cues that they alone could see that would help them become the person they want to be.

Our values are a large component of our authenticity. They make up our sense of self. That does not make it invincible. As we know all too well, it is easy to get distracted by success or searching for the right answers along the way and find ourselves distant from our values.

In the words of Mihaly Csikszentmihalyi, we keep some objects in view because "they tell us things about ourselves that we need to hear in order to keep ourselves from falling apart."

We've already discussed the dangers of holding too tightly to any one identity, especially when it is an external-facing identity. We can integrate cues in our spaces that help to define and cement all of our identities, especially the ones that reflect the most authentic versions of ourselves.

Daphna Oyserman, a psychologist at the University of Southern California, has noted that signals from the environment around us can bring our different identities to the forefront. With our different identities, we can tap into motivations and behaviors. Research has shown that cues reminding Asian American girls of their ethnicity improve their performance on math tests while cues reminding them of their gender have the opposite effect.

Placing meaningful material objects where we will encounter them regularly is a form of environmental self-regulation. We can use them to directly influence our moods, emotions, and behaviors. For example, incorporating personal items in the workspace can relieve the emotional exhaustion of a stressful job.

We can become intentional and experiment with different objects as we create an environment that supports the sustainable life we desire.

Give It Space

Beyond sleep, which gives our brain an opportunity to rewire and cleanse itself, other downtime is just as critical to give the brain space to do the work we are asking of it. Not all of our brains' power is accessed when we are consciously using it.

As analytical individuals, we love to see our brains working. We love to think hard and challenge ourselves with more and more complex puzzles. Ironically, to get the most benefit from our brains and face those complex puzzles, we have to give them space to work. We cannot require our brains to be constantly on.

The space we need can be created through meditation, intentionally breaking away, or simply creating silence.

I am relatively new to and extremely inconsistent with the practice of meditation. I have seasons where I can go weeks or even months with daily meditation. But it is also very easy for me to fall off the wagon.

There are about as many ways to meditate as there are people practicing meditation. I've experimented with guided meditations, walking meditations, silent meditations, and meditations that focus on specific mantras. Based on those experiments, I firmly believe that the best one is the one that works for you today.

I find that for me the most effective meditations for me include an aspect of becoming aware of myself and my surroundings. I can then start focusing on my breathing. I don't worry too much about the thoughts that float in and out of my awareness. I've learned that I cannot completely silence those. Although I have also learned that I don't have to hold on to each one and inspect it for hours.

Whichever approach you choose to experiment with, the goal is to reap some of the benefits of mindfulness and presence.

Meditation has been associated with many emotional benefits. The most common one is stress reduction. It can also lead to an improved self-image and a more positive outlook on life.

In one study, individuals that reflected deeply on their core values during meditation were able to see a future threat as a challenge and not simply a stressor. This enabled them to respond more productively to the threat. Meditation enabled participants to turn down the automatic response system of fight or flight.

During meditation and the opportunity for self-inquiry that it can offer, we can learn more about ourselves and more clearly see patterns materializing in our habits and thoughts. By practicing regular meditation, we can lengthen our attention spans and improve our sleep.

Meditation can break the cycle of the fast pace we are living at. The success we enjoy in our careers is often the direct result of the hard work and extra effort we put in. The promotions we enjoy are proof that we are achieving good things. When we spend long periods pushing hard at work, it can be difficult to turn that focus off. Our minds are often still mulling over the challenges at work even when we are technically off the clock. Mindfulness meditations can create a break in our thinking. It can offer the space to slow down and notice what our bodies are trying to tell us, especially when the subtle signs of burnout start to appear.

As accessible and flexible as meditation is, it can be used as a tool throughout your day to refocus your mind or distinctly separate phases of your work and your personal lives. Experiment with it to see what works best for you in different situations.

Practicing gratitude as a part of your meditation or on its own is another powerful tool.

When we express gratitude our brain releases dopamine and serotonin, which enhance our mood. When practiced daily, these neural pathways are strengthened and can become long-lasting states.

Gratitude redirects our brains to pay attention to what we have, which can produce intrinsic motivation and more clarity around what is true about our current situations.

Many people use gratitude journals to guide and capture their expressions of gratitude. Writing about a positive event we have experienced allows our brain to relive the experience and it has been seen to release the same chemicals associated with the initial positive experience. We can instill a recurring impact on our brains by expressing gratitude for what we appreciate in our lives.

Especially when we focus on events and experiences that we are grateful for, as opposed to outcomes and achievements, we are encouraging our brain to focus on the journey. We are training it to pay less attention to our specific achievements, which reduces the chance that we will get stuck in the success trap.

The final aspect of enabling your brain for its best work on your path of sustainability is to offer space at strategic times. Backing off instead of leaning into the challenge can trigger a powerful biological switch that increases mental function, creativity, and productivity. This concept is the breakout principle.

The hardest thing for many of us to do when we are close to discovering the breakthrough we have been chasing is to stop pushing. Stop demanding that the answer shows up in front of us. Yet breaking away from the problem is exactly what we might need.

More stress at some point becomes counterproductive. We often fail to see this when we have been sitting with the stress of a challenge for a while.

For analytical individuals, even when we are looking for insights that will help us create a sustainable life, we do so by taking in data and looking for patterns. We are relying on insights to appear that we can act on and experiment with. Those insights won't always develop when we are consciously looking for them.

We need to take our minds off the specific challenge for a while. We permit ourselves to go off work mode. Stop consciously trying to solve the challenge. Once we do that, we arrive at a place where the creative insights happen. An unanticipated new idea pops into our heads.

We don't have to meditate for this to happen. But we do need to create space. When we are experimenting with new things in our lives, take time to quiet the mind and stop consciously thinking about what we are learning from this experiment. Let the ideas come to us rather than chasing them.

It is through small and significant changes that we can set our brains up to be partners in our sustainable lives.

Analyze This...

1. Take 10 minutes each day to meditate or practice deep breathing exercises. Experiment with guided meditations, music, and locations to create a habit that you can maintain. There is no right answer in meditation. Identify a practice that feels comfortable for yourself.

2. Create an environment that reminds you of your strengths, values, and motivators. Do an audit of your work area and add, remove, or move items as necessary.

3. Build in space in the calendar to unplug. Schedule tech-free breaks to allow your brain space for reflection and sorting out recent thoughts.

CONCLUSION

Sustainability is simple. You've probably said it to yourself as you were reading this book. I think the same thing. But it is not easy. If it were, we would all already be living sustainable lives. We would not be suffering from the challenges of burnout and checking out or falling into the traps of our success and limiting identities.

Sustainability is found in three simple elements.

Show up authentically.

Be intentional in your choices and experiments.

And help your brain – your best friend – to help you along the way.

What you do with this information from here is up to you. Put it together in a framework that will guide you as you create sustainability in your life. Pick out the areas you are most curious about and learn more - there are many great books in the further reading section to let you do just that.

What you do with it is as unique as you are. I'm not here to hand you a model but to encourage you to create one that works for you today. Challenge yourself to make it easier for you to maintain the clarity of what you want, who you are, and keep yourself in motion.

Having grown up well before any smartphones or interactive maps were available, I learned to navigate using paper maps. Yes, the one that would never refold into its original shape once it was unfolded. While these maps got me around perfectly well in the past, they do not age well.

I came across a few of those maps recently. For fun, I opened them up to see what information they held (and for the challenge of refolding them). I found that what was true when the map was drawn is now outdated. There has been new growth in many areas. Many roads have come, and some have even gone. I am sure I would get lost if I relied on some of the older maps.

A map is a model of a specific location. It is meant to help guide and direct us when we find ourselves in that space. But a static map or model can quickly become outdated.

That does not mean that a map is not a good idea. It simply means we have to be flexible on how we build and maintain them.

As I create my own sustainable life and career, I use the clarity of my authenticity as a lens. By knowing who I am, the values that are important to me, the skills I want to be using today, and even the natural strength I am equipped with, I can see any situation I am in more clearly.

When I look closely, I can see multiple options in front of me for my career and personal life. In each of these paths forward, I can see some which allow me to stay in my comfort zone and others that will push me to grow by stretching my skills. I can see other paths that would demand too much of my energy and lead me far from what is important to me.

Whichever experiment I choose next, I know I will be walking it out with both my brain and my heart in mind. I am well equipped to create the sustainable life I have been missing out on.

And so are you.

RESOURCES: FURTHER READING

Throughout the shaping of this book, as it went from the twinkling of an idea to a fully-fledged work, I was constantly consuming the ideas of others, whether in books, podcasts, articles, or conversations. Since this book is simply a guide, it has only scratched the surface of many of the topics. The following books are here for you to explore if you find yourself wanting to go deeper.

There are so many books that could be included in this section. This is by no means an all-inclusive list. Rather it is a place to start as you dig into some of the ideas that resonated most with me as I wrote the book, or explore the concepts as you wrestle with the various challenges that arise as you begin creating a sustainable life and career.

As you will see, many books have overlapping themes. I include them to offer options for digging deep. Find the ones that speak to you.

Of course, books are not the only source. I encourage you to seek out podcasts and articles that highlight these authors and similar topics as well. Experiment to find the way you most like to learn so you can implement some of the ideas for yourself.

AUTHENTICITY

You Do You-ish

By Erin Hatzikostas

This is a practical guide for anyone that wants to have a more authentic and fulfilling career. Erin draws on her own experience as a successful corporate executive and entrepreneur (who was once on an actuarial path). She also pulls in insights from experts in psychology, personal development, and leadership.

Authenticity and success are not only not mutually exclusive, but we can achieve both through intentional alignment with our values and priorities. She reinforces my own experience of discovering the importance of putting core values at the center of our authenticity so they can be used as a guide for making decisions and setting goals.

She pushes the idea of embracing imperfections and taking risks, which is at the heart of experimenting along a sustainable path. With a series of guiding principles, or "isms," readers are encouraged to prioritize their own needs and values.

With a very conversational feel, I felt like we were sharing a coffee as she shared her stories. Not overly academic, but fun and insightful throughout. She even includes a range of exercises and tools to use in order to apply the principles of the book to your own career.

Daring Greatly

By Brené Brown

Daring Greatly is one of many fantastic books that Brené Brown has written under the broad category of vulnerability. In this one, she explores the idea that embracing vulnerability can lead to greater connection, courage, and fulfillment in life. To truly connect with others and live a wholehearted life, we must be willing to take risks, be vulnerable, and own our imperfections. We must be authentic.

The book is organized around themes including the importance of vulnerability, shame, resilience, and empathy as Brown draws from psychology and sociology research. By viewing vulnerability as a source of strength, we find it easier to step into that space in our many roles at work and home.

This is a well-written and thought-provoking book that offers new perspectives on vulnerability and connection. Her arguments are grounded in research and personal experience, and are offered in inspiring and actionable messages.

As an analytical individual that loves to find the right answers and is still working on developing the ability to find less shame in failures, I love her perspective.

Range

By David Epstein

I loved this book as it fits well with my jack-of-all-trades history (and present). While I appreciate Malcolm Gladwell's idea of the 10,000 hours required to become an outlier and truly excel in anything, this book was just the encouragement I needed.

Range challenges the notion that specialization is the only path to success. While deep expertise can be beneficial, there is a lot of value in the breadth of experiences as well. Even when we don't see immediate connections, our intuition can use that breadth to show us amazing opportunities.

The first part of the book explores the advantages of developing a range of skills and experiences. He notes the benefits of generalists in organizations as they bring new perspectives and problem-solving skills to the table. Citing diverse examples from sports, music, and science, Epstein shows how real people have excelled using their range.

The second part of the book looks at developing a range of skills and experiences. He emphasizes the importance of experimentation and exploration and suggests that we constantly seek out new challenges and experiences.

I love that he emphasizes that there is no one "right" path to success. It is a wilderness out there and we can benefit from charting a varied course as we explore different opportunities and paths.

This is a valuable read for anyone interested in personal development and career success. Using his ideas, we can increase our authenticity, adaptability, and resilience, and be better prepared to create more sustainable success in an ever-changing world.

Effortless

By Greg McKeown

As a follow-up to Essentialism (described later in this resource list), Effortless explores the concept of achieving more by doing less. We can find a state of flow in which we can accomplish what we want without the stress and struggles we are accustomed to. McKeown shifts the focus from working harder and sacrificing our health and happiness in favor of working smarter.

The focus is on leveraging the strengths we already have – hello, authenticity. By zeroing in on those and eliminating or delegating the rest to others, we can even create more space for rest and recovery which is vital to our well-being.

McKeown also ties into the importance of aligning with our values and interests in order to find more joy and make the work feel less like work. When we know what our values are, we can access the deeper meaning and sense of mission in our activities.

Through creating simplicity in the complex, we can guide ourselves to greater ease and effectiveness - both hallmarks of a more sustainable path. Effortless offers research-based insights and real-world examples.

I was struck by how similar an effortless life is to a sustainable life. Whichever word you prefer to use, the bottom line is creating more ease and more joy in life. In an effortless life, we are focused on managing our energy and understanding the importance of rest in recovery so we can recharge and ultimately increase our ability to be productive. McKeown also suggests that simplifying our lives is an important part of the equation.

CHOICE AND NAVIGATING

Stop Living on Autopilot

By Antonio Neves

Neves draws on touching and relatable stories from his own experience to bring to heart the importance of living with your heart. In Stop Living on Autopilot, we are being called out for our tendency to put our relationships and our careers on autopilot, allowing them to soften. This is the ultimate form of checking out.

He encourages readers to take control of all aspects of their lives by developing self-awareness, setting clear intentions, and taking action to make changes. He has many thought-provoking questions and exercises to help identify values, passions, and purpose.

Founded on the importance of developing meaningful relationships and connecting with others, Neves offers tips to cultivate empathy, communicate effectively, and build trust. These are all skills we can explore and strengthen in both personal and work environments.

The latter part of the book focuses on developing a growth mindset and taking action toward your goals. In that process, we can embrace failure, learn from setbacks, and stay committed to a vision. He offers many strategies for overcoming procrastination, building momentum, and creating a supportive environment.

This book is an excellent resource for anyone who feels stuck in a rut and wants to break free from feeling checked out of the best parts of their lives. It is a great handbook for creating an intentional and fulfilling life.

Better Than Destiny

By Frederic Bahnson

In Better Than Destiny, Bahnson offers insights and a framework for using choice to create the life you want. His insights were found in his journey. On his path, he discovered a sense of purpose and connection that had originally been missing in his life.

It wasn't in following his destiny, but rather in following his interests and making choices aligned with his values, that brought him to the life he loves. He emphasizes the importance of connecting with nature and offers evidence of the ways this connection can lead to greater fulfillment in our individual lives.

He shares wonderful insight into why our good brains make bad decisions. So many of our choices are influenced by hidden biases that are acting without us even being aware. We come by these biases honestly as humans. But they are not helping us to create sustainable and fulfilling lives.

Bahnson breaks down clear steps that we can follow to make better choices. The framework he offers is backed by science and extensive research. This is a practical and actionable guide for taking back control of our destiny.

Wild Problems

By Russ Roberts

Decision making is a challenge for me – as evidenced by not making a decision on which book on the theme of making decisions to include. Yes, the decisions we face that impact our lives are wild problems, indeed.

By tackling and talking about some of the big challenges we face today, from climate change to resource depletion, we start to understand the difficulty of solving these using traditional analytical approaches.

Roberts pulls from research in economics, ecology, and other fields to offer a range of real-world examples and case studies. He emphasizes the importance of understanding the incentives that drive human behavior. And he notes that we can design systems to encourage people and organizations to act in ways that promote sustainability.

Overall, this is a wonderfully well-written book that offers a new perspective on some of the immense societal challenges we face.

What surprised me is how frequently I could find ways to apply the same ideas on a smaller scale to my own decision-making. It helped me to understand the wild problem of creating a sustainable and fulfilling life for myself. It was a great book to shift my mind from strictly analytical thinking to a better approach for the nebulous challenges we face.

Think Again

By Adam Grant

As someone who loves to learn, it was kind of surprising that a book that focuses on the ability to unlearn would offer so many insights. As we navigate our careers and lives, however, it is more important than ever that we keep our minds open and willing to revise our beliefs in light of what we discover along the way. Being able to think again about any topic in our lives is essential for both personal and professional growth.

Grant introduces the concept of cognitive flexibility. This is our ability to shift our thinking in changing circumstances. In today's unpredictable world, it can be the key to success.

His idea of motivated reasoning speaks to the tendency of our biases to look for evidence to support our existing beliefs. These biases can hold us in place and limit our learning and growth.

As in all his books, Grant offers many examples in case studies to illustrate his position. And he offers practical advice for cultivating a mindset of cognitive flexibility and methods to overcome the biases that prevent us from changing our minds today.

It is a wonderful roadmap for both personal and professional growth as we grapple with being wrong and with recognizing what we do not know. I definitely did not rethink including this book as an amazing resource.

Emotional Equations

By Chip Conley

This is a great resource for any math nerd. Conley presents a series of mathematical formulas designed to help individuals understand and manage their emotions. Based on experience as an entrepreneur and rooted in psychology and neuroscience research, he shows how emotions can be understood and managed using a structured, analytical approach.

The simple equations provide a framework for breaking down our emotions into their core components. For example, he suggests that happiness can be expressed as the sum of our natural baseline of happiness, the current conditions of our life, and our voluntary actions. Our disappointment is the difference between our expectations and our reality.

Each equation is accompanied by real-life examples, as well as practical strategies for managing the corresponding emotion. Looking at emotions in their component parts was integral for identifying some of the root causes of my own emotions.

Conley emphasizes the importance of emotional intelligence in both personal and professional contexts. By understanding our emotions and effectively managing them, we can improve our relationships, work performance, and overall well-being.

The personal anecdotes and vivid metaphors make the concepts relatable and easy to apply in our own lives. This is a great resource for anyone wanting to make sense of the emotional side of their experiences.

Essentialism

By Greg McKeown

Essentialism was the first book of Greg McKeown's that I discovered. In a world that is battling to take every ounce of our attention and turn it toward what is important to everyone around us, but not to ourselves, this book explores the importance of focusing on what is truly important and eliminating distractions for ourselves.

To take ourselves out of an unfulfilling and overwhelming life, we can discern what matters and dedicate our energy and resources to those things.

McKeown emphasizes the need to prioritize and say no to non-essential tasks. He offers a framework for making decisions by asking whether an opportunity aligns with one's goals and values as well as considering the time and effort it requires. He even stresses the importance of creating space for reflection to help gain clarity about what you want and how to choose a good path in that direction.

A key insight about essentialism is that it is not only about productivity but also about living a meaningful and fulfilling life. McKeown encourages readers to focus on their unique talents and interests.

This is a fantastic book for anyone feeling overwhelmed or directionless in their career or life. His approach is, as always, practical and accessible.

SUPPORTING YOUR BRAIN

The Extended Mind

By Annie Murphy Paul

This was one of the most interesting books I have stumbled upon lately. It broadened my understanding of how we think. How our minds work. We tend to think of the brain as a tool that works independently, standing alone in the powerful position in our skulls. The extended mind showed me so many ways our minds are connected to our bodies and the world around us.

The book explores three main areas of cognition. The first is the concept of embodied cognition in which the body and our environment play a crucial role in shaping our thinking and perception. Our thoughts and actions are not just the result of the brain's activity, but also of the body's interaction with the environment.

Extended cognition is the idea that our mind is not just confined to our brain and body but is also impacted by external objects and tools that help us to think and solve problems. There are ways we can better utilize some of these to extend our cognitive abilities.

Finally, the book explores social cognition. In this respect, our thinking and behavior are shaped by our interactions with other people. Through communication, cooperation, and coordination, we can augment our cognitive development.

Murphy Paul provides numerous examples in case studies throughout the book. It is a wonderful and comprehensive perspective on how we think, learn, and interact with the world around us, enabling us to support our brain better for all that we ask of it.

Stress Less, Accomplish More

By Emily Fletcher

This book was my first foray into reading about meditation. I had dabbled before this with mixed results. Fletcher's approach to using the practice of meditation to reduce stress and increase productivity is geared toward finding practical benefits for busy professionals.

She offers a new approach to meditation that is designed to improve focus, creativity, and productivity. Ziva meditation includes mindfulness, meditation, and manifesting. Together, these help individuals become more aware of their thoughts and emotions, develop a sense of calm and focus, and set clear intentions and goals.

Fletcher includes plenty of studies to support the use of meditation as a way to improve focus and productivity as well as reduce stress. It isn't woo-woo science after all.

By providing a comprehensive approach to meditation and emphasizing the practical benefits, Fletcher offers a compelling case for incorporating this practice into our daily lives. While I do not always follow every element of her meditation each day, I have found this type of meditation to be very accessible to my analytical mind.

Drive

By Daniel Pink

I probably used up a full stack of post-it notes as I devoured this book. Drive explores the nature of human motivation and how it shows up in the modern workplace. Pink argues that motivation is driven by three key factors: autonomy, mastery, and purpose.

The book delves into extrinsic motivation in which fame, money, or praise are used to encourage an individual's actions and behaviors. Much of this type of motivation does not work in the workplace today. Instead, it focuses on the concept of intrinsic motivation in which people are motivated by internal factors of personal satisfaction, curiosity, and learning.

Pink offers many examples of companies and individuals that have successfully applied the principles of intrinsic motivation to achieve success. He shares practical advice for both individuals and organizations wanting to increase motivation and productivity.

His framework of building intrinsic motivation through autonomy, mastery, and purpose has worked for me and many colleagues and clients.

Drive challenges some of our long-held views of motivation and gives us a toolkit to use the ideas in many situations. It is a wonderful roadmap for creating more success and fulfillment in our work.

Flow

By Mihaly Csikszentmihalyi

This is one of the older books on the list. In it, Csikszentmihalyi introduces and explores the concept of "flow" as he argues that this state is essential for happiness and fulfillment.

Flow is the state of consciousness in which we are fully absorbed in an activity, lose track of time, and experience a sense of enjoyment and accomplishment. It offers insights into achieving flow in different areas of life. Flow is one way in which we can help our brain create a sustainable path.

There are many factors that contribute to experiencing flow, including ensuring that the right balance of challenge and skill is found, using clear goals and feedback, and having a sense of control over the activity. The book offers many examples and case studies of flow in work, sports, and creative endeavors.

Csikszentmihalyi also explores the role of culture and social context in creating flow, and how we can foster and encourage flow in various environments. He emphasizes the importance of mindfulness and self-awareness in achieving flow.

When able to create flow, we can enjoy many benefits including improved performance, creativity, and well-being.

As the first book on flow, this offers a wonderful base understanding of the importance and role of flow in creating a fulfilling life. Although it is not the last book on flow (Steven Kotler is a more contemporary author, podcaster, and thought leader on the topic, and well worth looking up as well), it is a great opportunity to start exploring at the ground level.

Atomic Habits

By James Clear

Clear offers a powerful book that is sure to change your habits. He focuses on the process of habit formation rather than only the outcome. Many of the principles he offers are simple tools for anyone creating a sustainable life. Through breaking down large goals and creating a system for consistently implementing the small building blocks, we can develop habits that lead to long-term and sustainable success.

Creating the right environment that can support our habits is an important element. Whether we are focused on our physical or social environments, we can set ourselves up for easier paths to wherever we want to go using Clear's guidance.

Of course, the book helps us to understand and identify some of the underlying beliefs and motivations that have kept us from developing strong (and positive) habits in the past. It is only when we can see these factors that we can effectively change our behaviors today and develop new habits that can carry us effortlessly ahead.

Atomic Habits is a very practical and actionable guide for developing positive habits that will be a powerful secret weapon for creating your sustainable future in all areas of life.

The Happiness Advantage

By Shawn Achor

Happiness and success are integrally connected, but not in the way we tend to think. The Happiness Advantage flips the script on success as Achor argues that happiness is what leads to success rather than the other way around. By cultivating a positive mindset and being present in the moment, we can find more happiness and success in both professional and personal lives. Isn't that what sustainability is all about?

Achor digs into many principles of happiness that are also keys to creating a sustainable life. Some of these are gratitude, social connection and relationships, and mindfulness. He pulls from research in many fields to support his ideas and offers many practical exercises for readers to use as they explore the principles in their own lives.

It is the practical application that I found most helpful in the book. With the strategies and tools that Achor offers, we can all make changes today.

Achor's writing style is both entertaining and informational. This new perspective on happiness is grounded in solid research. The beautiful thing about happiness is that it is contagious. As you apply these principles in your own life, don't be surprised to see it creating a ripple effect on those around you.

GENERAL SUSTAINABILITY

The Practice of Groundedness

By Brad Stulberg

Groundedness is a necessary element of sustainability. Without a solid foundation, we will not easily find a sustainable path. Stulberg's book offers a practical guide for building resilience, finding emotional stability, and more easily managing life's ups and downs.

Through research in psychology, neuroscience, and mindfulness, he offers principles and exercises that readers can use to ground themselves in their lives.

Organized around four principles that include presence, purpose, perspective, and persistence, Stulberg gives us the basic tools to ground our own lives. With an ability to find more inner calm, focus, and resilience, we can equip ourselves to make it through the inevitable times of stress and adversity more comfortably.

Stulberg spends some time sharing both the importance of and ways to practice mindfulness through meditation and breathwork. Some of the exercises he offers will support your ability to find sustainability in your own life. Whether journaling, visualization, or through gratitude, we can learn to influence our own emotions and self-awareness.

The real-world examples and strategies are easy to apply and offered through engaging storytelling. This is a great guide to get started developing a more grounded experience for yourself.

Big Potential

By Shawn Achor

Sustainability is not something we are going to achieve on our own. We need the support of others and to be the support for others.

Big Potential explores how harnessing the power of social support and collaboration can unlock some of the happiness in our lives. Achor offers extensive research examples and real-world scenarios that demonstrate the power of collective potential.

Each of the sections addresses a different aspect of social support and collaboration. The first section explores positive social connections. These relationships have a significant positive impact on our success and well-being.

Positive team dynamics and developing a culture of collaboration are elements of happiness. These can be supported through gratitude and acts of kindness.

In the final section on social contagion, Achor shows us how our behaviors and attitudes are influenced by those around us. We can better create a sustainable life for ourselves when we put ourselves in contact with others that will positively impact our path.

The book is the practical and research-based support to the adage that we can go farther together.

The Long Game

By Dorie Clark

The Long Game recognizes the need to adapt, innovate, and experiment as we create our unique fulfilling and sustainable future. We are here to play the long game, and we are best able to do that by investing in our development.

Clark focuses on the importance of a strategic vision and setting long-term goals, although she also encourages us to hold them appropriately. We can find paths toward those goals that align with our strengths, values, and interests.

In a complex and dynamic economy and workplace, our long-term success will require us to take risks (and experiment), adapt to change (know how we are changing as well), and constantly learn and grow.

The book is well-written and a joy to read. My analytical side enjoys all the case studies that she pulls from various industries to illustrate the ideas.

ACKNOWLEDGMENTS

This book was not written by me alone. Well, the words are mine. I will also take credit for the page numbers. The book would never have become a reality if not for the love and encouragement from so many others.

The ideas and concepts in the book were inspired, supported, envisioned, and egged along by too many people for me to name. Here are just a few.

To my husband and partner in life, Tom, you support me in so many of my harebrained ideas. Thank you for taking on more so that I could spend time on this book. But mostly thank you for believing in me and this completely out of my comfort zone endeavor.

To my girls Delia, Gabi, and Lara, thank you for inspiring me to live true to who I am every day. To find humor in the challenges. I have been blessed to be your mom and cannot wait to see what else you will teach me.

To all of the individuals that have taken time to sit down and talk with me about your experiences. I am indebted to you. You helped bring the book to life in ways that will resonate with many more people than I could have alone. Whether your stories were shared directly or only in spirit, I appreciate your openness in allowing me into the ups and downs of your own sustainable lives.

To Kevin who put the bug in my ear in the first place and added the "creative" to my writing process. You were the perfect balance to my analytical mind.

To Lise who led me through the final processes of birthing a book. You simplified it all to the point of making it look and feel easy.

To all the authors of the books I explicitly named as resources, and the many other thought leaders that I have not named whether authors of books or articles, hosts of podcasts, or deliverers of TED/TEDx talks. There are so many great conversations happening in so many formats around these ideas. Thank you for sharing your wisdom with the world.

ABOUT THE AUTHOR

What fuels Aree's passion for living a sustainable life herself and helping others do the same is the profound joy that comes from making the most of our limited time on this earth. Having learned from a young age just how fragile life can be, she believes we all have a responsibility to pay closer attention and navigate our journeys with intention, purpose, and joy.

With a wealth of experience as an actuary, certified coach, and speaker, Aree combines her analytical prowess with a deep understanding of human dynamics and personal growth. As an ally to others, she empowers analytical professionals to create sustainable and fulfilling careers.

Whether she's speaking at conferences, leading workshops, or working one-on-one with clients, Aree's approach is rooted in compassion, curiosity, and a genuine desire to see others succeed. Oh, and a little adventure as well, which is what has taken her to the TEDx stage and motivated her to shift from numbers to words for a book.

Aree's commitment to sustainability extends beyond her professional endeavors. She believes that a sustainable life encompasses not only career success but also personal well-being and a deep connection with the world around us. Drawing inspiration from her love of nature and adventure, she encourages others to embrace a life filled with purpose, growth, and meaningful connections.

You can often find her on the tennis court, in the mountains, petting bees in the backyard, or traveling to learn about other cultures and people.

As of the publishing of this book, there are a few courses and other fun surprises under development. Check her website or reach out by email to learn more.

Visit www.alignmentally.com for coaching or www.areebly.com for speaking and workshop information.

Find her on LinkedIn as Aree Bly (how's that for authenticity?).

Reach out via email at Aree@AlignmentAlly.com

www.ingramcontent.com/pod-product-compliance
Lightning Source LLC
Chambersburg PA
CBHW071554210326
41597CB00019B/3237